1979

Andalusian Lyrical Poetry and Old Spanish Love Songs

NEW YORK UNIVERSITY

STUDIES IN NEAR EASTERN CIVILIZATION

NUMBER 6

General Editors
R. Bayly Winder
Richard Ettinghausen

ALSO IN THIS SERIES

Number I: F. E. Peters, Aristotle and the Arabs

Number II: Jacob M. Landau, Jews in Nineteenth-Century Egypt

Number III: Lois Anita Giffen, Theory of Profane Love Among the Arabs: The Development of the Genre

Number IV: Lewis V. Thomas, A Study of Naima
Norman Itzkowitz, editor

Number V: Carl Max Kortepeter, Ottoman Imperialism During the Reformation: Europe and The Caucasus

Andalusian Lyrical Poetry and Old Spanish Love Songs:

The *Muwashshaḥ* and its *Kharja*

Linda Fish Compton

New York: New York University Press · 1976

Library of Congress Catalog Card Number: 74-21597
ISBN: 0-8147-1359-9

Library of Congress Cataloging in Publication Data

Compton, Linda Fish, 1940–
Andalusian lyrical poetry and old Spanish love songs.

Bibliography: p.
Includes index.
1. Muwashshah. I. Title.
PJ7542.M8C6 892'.7'104 74-21597
ISBN 0-8147-1359-9

Manufactured in the United States of America

For Randall and Key

Preface

Although the medieval Spanish love songs, known as *kharjas*, have been the subject of research and debate since their discovery in 1948, relatively little is known about the lovely strophic poems, called *muwashshaḥs*, in which they are contained. Because the *kharjas* are the oldest known secular lyrics in any Romance language, they occupy a significant position within the mainstream of Western lyrical poetry. The exact relationship of these lyrics to the poetry of Europe and the Middle East has not been clearly determined, however. When trying to deal with this problem, most Westerners have had limited access to the original texts of the *muwashshaḥs*, which were composed in classical Arabic. Except for a few isolated examples, the *muwashshaḥs* have not been translated. In an effort to fill this gap, I decided to prepare an English translation of an outstanding Andalusian anthology, compiled by Ibn Sanā' al-Mulk (d. 1211). Readers who are unfamiliar with Arabic would then be able to consult the source.

In order to arrive at a better understanding of the Andalusian *muwashshaḥ* and its *kharja*, I have divided my attention between Ibn Sanā' al-Mulk's Arabic anthology and a comparable collection of bilingual poems whose *kharjas* were written in Mozarabic, the Romance dialect of Muslim Spain. In Part I (Chapters I–III), I have focused on the Arabic *muwashshaḥs*, discussing them in terms of theory and content. Part II (Chapters IV–VI), consists of a comparative study of the Arabic and bilingual poems, which is a necessary step in any attempt to establish their cultural identity. Pertinent passages of the bilingual *muwashshaḥs* have been translated into English, along with many of the Mozarabic *kharjas*. In the Appendix, I have presented a brief historical sketch for those who are interested in the cultural crosscurrents which may have influenced the development of this genre. Needless to say, many questions remain unanswered, and I look forward to reading the interpretations of others in the future.

While working on this project, I benefited immeasurably from the assistance given me by R. S. Willis, Philip K. Hitti, and Andras Hamori. I am also very grateful to James T. Monroe for his valuable suggestions. Although I can not thank everyone individually, I would like to acknowledge my indebtedness to Emilio García Gómez and the late Samuel M. Stern for their excellent pioneering efforts in this field and to the many scholars listed in the bibliography, for I consider them among my teachers. Regrettably, I only received a copy of J. M. Solá-Solé's *Corpus de poesía mozárabe* in time to incorporate some of his fine insights in the form of brief notes to Chapter VI. In addition to these scholars, I would like to express my gratitude to the Andrew W. Mellon Foundation for its aid in the publication of this book. Finally, I owe a special vote of thanks to my husband, Beverley, who had the patience to accept the long hours connected with this work.

SYSTEM OF TRANSLITERATION

Arabic Letter	Name of Arabic Letter	Transcription
ا	'alif	ā
ب	bā'	b
ت	tā'	t
ث	thā'	th
ج	jīm	j
ح	ḥā'	ḥ
خ	khā'	kh
د	dāl	d
ذ	dhāl	dh
ر	rā'	r
ز	zāy	z
س	sīn	s
ش	shīn	sh
ص	ṣād	ṣ
ض	ḍād	ḍ
ط	ṭā'	ṭ
ظ	ẓā'	ẓ
ع	ᶜain	ᶜ
غ	ghain	gh
ف	fā'	f
ق	qāf	q
ك	kāf	k
ل	lām	l
م	mīm	m
ن	nūn	n
ه	hā'	h
و	wāw	w (ū, aw, au)
ى	yā'	y (ī, ay, ai)
ء	hamza	'

Contents

Introduction

The lyrical poetry featured in this book originated in Muslim Spain during the Middle Ages and eventually spread throughout North Africa and the Middle East, where it is still popular today. These strophic poems, called *muwashshaḥs*, were composed mainly in Arabic, which was the primary language of the region. When the Muslim armies overran most of Spain at the beginning of the eighth century, however, they encountered people speaking a Romance dialect which had evolved from Vulgar Latin. After Arabic, this Romance dialect, which came to be known as Mozarabic, remained the second language spoken by Christians, Jews, and Muslims who lived in the area. In 1948, Samuel M. Stern discovered lyrical fragments of this archaic language, preserved in Arabic script, at the end of bilingual *muwashshaḥs* which date back to the eleventh century.[1] These brief but beautiful verses are known as *kharjas*, an Arabic term which designates the *muwashshaḥ*'s final lines. Poets and scholars alike were excited about Stern's disclosure, for he had uncovered the oldest known examples of secular poetry in a vernacular Romance language. Since then, a spotlight has been turned on the *kharjas*, which form a small yet important part of each *muwashshaḥ* and contribute to its elegant complexity.

Hispanists have been doubly elated about these fascinating *kharjas* because they prove the existence of medieval lyrics in a Spanish dialect that was spoken in al-Andalus. This large area of the Iberian peninsula, extending from Gibraltar to the Pyrenees, includes all but the northernmost regions of Spain, where a number of Visigoths who fled from the invading Arabs maintained a separate culture. Al-Andalus, therefore, indicates all the Iberian territory under Muslim domination and not just the area of southern Spain now commonly called Andalusia. The extent of the Arabs' dominion can easily be seen in the names of various poets who composed *muwashshaḥs*. Geographical adjectives, which often form part of a Muslim name, reveal that the blind bard, al-Tuṭīlī, came from the northeastern town of Tudela and that al-Kumait al-Gharbī, also known as al-Baṭalyausī, was from the southwestern province of Algarve or the city of Badajoz.

Within the borders of al-Andalus, a highly diversified society flourished. Initially many people converted to the conqueror's religion, even though Islamic law did not require this. The Islamic code, in fact, was surprisingly tolerant. Many Christian women who married Arabs or Berbers, for instance, were not forced to convert, although their children were brought up within the Muslim fold. Due to such conversions and intermarriages, the Muslim community formed a majority of the population after the ninth century; but Christian and Jewish minorities that were unwilling to forsake their faith continued to live there. As in the rest of the Arab world, Islamic law was lenient enough to allow them to maintain their own cultural and ethnic identity. Nevertheless, the Christian minority became highly Arabized through daily contact with the ubiquitous majority. Through this process of adaptation, they became known as Mozarabs. This word is derived from the Arabic term, *mustaᶜrib*, a person who adopts the customs of the Arabs. Mozarabic, the name of the Romance dialect which they spoke, is derived from the same source.

Despite the extent to which these Christians absorbed the Arabic language and culture, their own language and religion did not disappear. Similar conditions prevailed among the Jews, who were greatly influenced by Arabic civilization. Both groups continued to worship in their own churches or synagogues, maintained separate law courts and judges, and existed as protected citizens within the dominating social structure of Islam. Neither Christians nor Jews were granted all the privileges of citizenship that a Muslim had, but they did enjoy a generous measure of autonomy.

Within this composite social framework, it should not be a great surprise to find poets composing bilingual lyrics in Arabic and Romance. Both languages were spoken there and bilingual citizens were found in all strata of society. Furthermore, Hebrew-speaking poets of the region followed the familiar Arabic models and wrote their own Hebrew *muwashshaḥs* with Mozarabic *kharjas* at the end. Such poets might belong to various social classes, but the main setting in which the *muwashshaḥ* flourished seems to have been the court. They were composed to be sung, as their strophic structure indicates, and were a popular form of entertainment. A quick glance at the content of these songs will also reveal that many of them must have been created specifically for rulers of the period and the courtly society which surrounded them. Panegyrics, wine songs, and sophisticated love lyrics all appealed to a refined and educated palate. To what extent *muwashshaḥs* were sung outside this elite environment is still undetermined, for the classical literary language which flows through all but the final *kharja* would have been appreciated and understood primarily by a literate, aristocratic audience.

Many fine commentaries have been written about the enigmatic *kharjas* since 1948, but it was not until 1965 that Emilio García Gómez published and translated a collection of complete Arabic *muwashshaḥs* in which the Romance *kharjas* appear.[2] While reading these, it occurred to me that we could learn more about the nature of the *muwashshaḥ* and its puzzling *kharja* if a similar group of *muwashshaḥs*, written totally in Arabic, could be studied and compared with the bilingual ones. Through the process of analysis and contrast, both the *muwashshaḥ* and its *kharja* would be brought into sharper focus. In the course of this study, for example, basic similarities between the main part of the Arabic and bilingual *muwashshaḥs* became evident. Significant differences in thematic content and voice also appeared at the end of the poems: The Mozarabic *kharjas* are love lyrics which are almost always sung by women, whereas the Arabic poems collected by Ibn Sanā' al-Mulk rarely introduce the feminine voice and often feature panegyrics or ascetic themes instead of love.

Questions concerning early Spanish, Provençal, and Galician-Portuguese poetry may be linked to the *muwashshaḥ*'s obscure origins. The *kharjas*, which contain feminine lyrics, or *cantigas de ḥabīb*, may be related to the French *chansons à danser*, the *cantigas de amigo* of the Iberian peninsula, or even the German *frauenleider*. In this book, however, I have not constructed a genealogy of this lyrical form nor a theory of how the *muwashshaḥ* is related to European lyrics or Arabic poetry, to which it is closely bound. Instead I have concentrated on translating Ibn Sanā' al-Mulk's anthology of Andalusian Arabic *muwashshaḥs* into English, gathering relevant information from Arabic sources, and comparing these Arabic poems with bilingual Arabic-Romance *muwashshaḥs* from the manuscripts of Ibn Bushrā and Ibn al-Khaṭīb, which García Gómez has carefully transliterated and translated into Spanish. In this way, I have been able to present the Arabic *kharjas* in context as part of a larger and equally important whole. By using Ibn Sanā' al-Mulk's examples as a general guide, which he fully intended them to be, it is possible to contrast them with *muwashshaḥs* containing Romance elements, thereby providing a fresh perspective.

Ibn Sanā' al-Mulk, who lived in Egypt during the late twelfth century, not only compiled an anthology of eleventh- and twelfth-century Andalusian Arabic *muwashshaḥs*, but he also formulated a theory of how they should be written, based on observation of all the *muwashshaḥs* to which he had access. Both are found in his book, *Dār al-Ṭirāz* (*The House of Embroidery*), published in 1949 by Jawdat Rikābī in an adequate edition which I have chosen for my basic text.[3] In his anthology, there are thirty-four *muwashshaḥs*. This balances nicely with the bilingual *muwashshaḥs*, which have a total of thirty-eight Mozarabic *kharjas* culled by García Gómez from manuscripts compiled by two fourteenth-century authors from Granada: *Jaish al-Tawshīḥ* by Lisān al-Dīn ibn al-Khaṭīb al-Salmānī and ᶜ*Uddat al-jalīs wa mu'ānasat al-wazīr wa al-ra'īs* by ᶜAli ibn Bushrā al-Ighranāṭī.[4] The poets included in these collections lived during the period when Muslim Spain's literary culture was flourishing, and four of the identifiable poets in *Dār al-Ṭirāz* wrote *muwashshaḥs* with Mozarabic *kharjas* that were found in the two above-mentioned manuscripts. The four poets are Ibn Baqī, Ibn al-Labbāna, al-Aᶜmā al-Tuṭīlī, and the problematical Ibn ᶜUbāda.[5] I should also mention that there is some overlapping of poets in the texts of Ibn Bushrā and Ibn al-Khaṭīb, even though this is not particularly important for the present study. Bilingual *muwashshaḥs* by Ibn Baqī, Ibn Ruhaym, al-Khabbāz al-Mursī, and al-Kumait al-Gharbī have been included in both compilations.

In order to avoid confusing references to the published texts, I have retained the original numerals employed in each. Rikābī used Arabic numerals in *Dār al-Ṭirāz*, whereas García Gómez has given each bilingual *muwashshaḥ* a Roman numeral. Poems from Ibn Bushrā's collection are numbered I through XXVI, and those taken from Ibn al-Khaṭīb include Nos. XXVII through XXXVIII. Only two *muwashshaḥs*, Nos. VIII and XXIIb, are found in both manuscripts. In cases of doubtful authorship, I have relied on García Gómez's experienced judgment and accepted his attributions.

When discussing many of the problems involved with these medieval Mozarabic *kharjas* and Arabic *muwashshaḥs*, we can only speak of possibilities and probabilities. Too little is yet known for anyone to be dogmatically certain about their solutions. Besides a paucity of data, the few manuscripts in which *muwashshaḥs* are contained cannot be read with total accuracy due to physical impairments such as blurred letters or damage to the folios because of age and lack of care, in addition to the typical lack of vocalization and occasionally omitted diacritical marks which distinguish the consonants. Scribal error is another grave obstacle with which it is difficult to cope. In later centuries, Arabic-speaking scribes probably did not understand the Mozarabic dialect, so they could have confused the strange words they encountered in a number of ways. Even when the language was familiar, scribes were capable of making innumerable errors, as anyone who has worked with medieval source material well knows. When it comes to figuring out scribal errors, it is helpful to have several versions or copies of the same text. In this case, scholars consider themselves lucky to have one extant manuscript at their disposal. Furthermore, contemporary knowledge of the Mozarabic dialect is sufficiently limited to reduce many readings to educated guesses. The interpretations, therefore, may vary widely.

Similar difficulties exist in regard to Ibn Sanā' al-Mulk's Andalusian anthology, which I have translated from Arabic into English. First of all, the text of *Dār al-Ṭirāz* is not voweled. Secondly, the exact definition of Arabic words as they were used in Spain is often hard to ascertain. The existence of regional variations is a common phenomenon, but because there are no linguistic informants to whom we can turn today, elements of doubt will continue to haunt Hispano-Arabists. As a result, perfect translations will remain an unattainable goal. On the other hand, many enigmatic lines and inaccuracies may be resolved in the future. Where my English versions of the bilingual *kharjas* are concerned, I would like to emphasize that I regard them as reconstructions rather than literal translations, because we are still uncertain about the exact letters in many lines, not to mention the precise translation after a correct reading is established.

In addition to these Andalusian *muwashshaḥs*, I have included background material gleaned from other Arabic sources and analytic commentary; but I have tried not to draw premature conclusions. In many instances, the use of certain basic Arabic terms was unavoidable. To simplify the problem of unfamiliar vocabulary, a glossary has been included. I have not discussed the corpus of bilingual Hebrew *muwashshaḥs*, which would have added a third cultural dimension, beyond the scope of this book; nor have I delved into the development of the *zajal*, a poetic form which resembles the *muwashshaḥ* in various ways and which is often mistaken for it.[6] My intention has been to increase our understanding of the Andalusian *muwashshaḥ* with its captivating *kharja* and to elucidate a number of fundamental similarities and differences between the Arabic and bilingual poems in question.

PART ONE

Andalusian *Muwashshaḥs*

CHAPTER ONE
Ibn Sanā' al-Mulk's Theory of the *Muwashshaḥ*

The first man, as far as we know, to study the *muwashshaḥ* seriously and write down the results of his analysis in a theoretical framework was not an Andalusian but an Egyptian, Ibn Sanā' al-Mulk, who lived from 1155 to 1211. He became addicted to *muwashshaḥs* as a young man and thoroughly familiarized himself with them. People who could not appreciate them as he did, he felt, must be lacking in artistic sensitivity and basic intelligence. So great was his love for this "modern form," more accurately described as post-classical, that upon finding nothing written about its fundamental characteristics, he decided to make such information his own contribution to the cultural realm. It would serve as a guide for those who wished to learn about the composition of *muwashshaḥs* in the future and would help those already familiar with the form to clarify various obscure aspects and solve problems that might arise concerning the poems. The resulting treatise, *Dār al-Ṭirāz* (The House of Embroidery), is concise and thorough.

Despite the fact that there are records of Arabic poetics and poetry from the ninth century, when the *muwashshaḥ* was invented, to the twelfth century, when Ibn Sanā al-Mulk was born, *muwashshaḥs* were not considered a legitimate form of poetic art. Most contemporary scholars would not even include examples of them in literary anthologies.[1] This undoubtedly contributed to the lack of theoretical knowledge concerning the composition of the new form. Literate Andalusians had been in a position to understand and contribute comprehensive information, if only they had deigned to do so. Their negative attitude does not seem to have interfered with the *muwashshaḥ*'s popularity, but it certainly added to future confusion about its source, development, and construction. Much has been lost due to this unfortunate prejudice, and it would be unrealistic to expect an Egyptian, who was born during the latter half of the twelfth century, to fit all the pieces together without ever having lived or traveled in al-Andalus and North Africa. We can, nonetheless, be grateful to Ibn Sanā' al-Mulk for providing us with a meticulous analysis of the *muwashshaḥ* and for all the information he accumulated and related as accurately as possible.

Other medieval authors, such as Ibn Bassām al-Shantarīnī or Ibn Khaldūn, have included discussions of the *muwashshaḥ*, but they are not as complete or comprehensive. Furthermore, the terms they use to describe the poem's structure differ from the ones chosen by Ibn Sanā' al-Mulk.[2] For the sake of clarity, therefore, I will adhere to Ibn Sanā' al-Mulk's set of terms which I have found to be satisfactory. Because García Gómez has already produced a fine Spanish translation of Ibn Sanā' al-Mulk's theoretical exposition,[3] I do not think that it is necessary or appropriate to repeat all of the material given there; but for those who are unfamiliar with either the original Arabic text or García Gómez's Spanish translation, a brief summary of his thought and terminology may be helpful.

Aesthetically, the *muwashshaḥ* scores very high in Ibn Sanā' al-Mulk's mind. He is thoroughly delighted that the "modern," or postclassical, poets have discovered it and imported it from the Maghrib. It is the essence of precious things to him: aloe-wood of India, magic of Babylon, fine wine from Qufs, amber, and gold. Intangibly, the *muwashshaḥ* is a measure of the mind. It stirs people to heights of joy or sadness; it can tempt and charm, amuse or fill us with aversion. When it seems serious, it may be a joke and when it seems to be a jest, it may be earnest. He expresses deep gratitude to the Occident for sharing this rich treasure with the Orient.

To form an idea of the esteem in which he held the *muwashshaḥ* and the painstaking care with which he prepared his treatise, it is worth paying attention to the explanation he gives for his choice of title, *Dār al-Ṭirāz* (The House of Embroidery). He tentatively thought of several others, such as "How the *Muwashshaḥ* is Made," or "Necklace of the *Muwashshaḥ*," but he rejected them all as inadequate. Only in the royal house of embroidery were the most beautiful, precious, and rare fabrics created, those woven in silk and gold thread, he explains. Hoping that his book would be as valuable, he selected a title which was meant to be a characteristic sign, symbolizing the contents' value.

Turning to the technical side of Ibn Sanā' al-Mulk's work, we find a clear analysis of the *muwashshaḥ*'s structure, along with concrete examples to illustrate each aspect. He describes the *muwashshaḥ* as a group of rhyming phrases molded into a pattern which consists of strophes that can be divided into parts called *qufls* and *baits*. *Bait* is a standard Arabic word for stanza; and *qufl* is a term derived from the triliteral root, *q-f-l*, which means "to return," thereby indicating the *qufl*'s function within the poem.[4] Six *qufls* and five *baits* form a complete (*tamm*) *muwashshaḥ*. In this case, the first *qufl* is called a *maṭla*^{c}, which means "opening verses." Sometimes the *maṭla*^{c} is omitted and there are only five *qufls* and *baits*. This produces a variation known as a bald (*aqra*^{c}) *muwashshaḥ*. He proceeds to specify that, within each poem, all *qufls* must match in meter, rhyme, and number of parts. *Baits* must have the same meter and number of parts but, with each repetition, they should contain a different rhyme. Usually there are anywhere from two to eight parts in each *qufl*. In the *bait*, there are three to five parts, although five is the more common number. The *qufl*, however, should always be simple and unbroken, whereas the *bait*'s verses may be either simple or composite and divided into two or three parts (more rarely into four). What Ibn Sanā' al-Mulk does not mention is the possibility of syntactical unity between a *bait* and its subsequent *qufl*, which appears whenever a phrase begins in the *bait* and terminates in the *qufl*. To enable the reader to visualize this easily, I will arrange a few examples schematically. The simplest *muwashshaḥ* would conform to the following diagram:

opening *qufl* ____________Y
or *maṭla*^{c}: ____________Z

____________________A
bait: ____________________A
____________________A

qufl: ____________Y
____________Z

(The alternating *bait* and *qufl* pattern is repeated three times.)

final strophe:

____________________E
bait: ____________________E
____________________E

last *qufl* ____________Y
or *kharja*: ____________Z

A more complicated *muwashshaḥ* might be set up this way.

opening *qufl* ____________W
or *maṭla*^{c}: ____________X
____________Y
____________Z

____________A ____________B
____________A ____________B
bait: ____________A ____________B
____________A ____________B
____________A ____________B

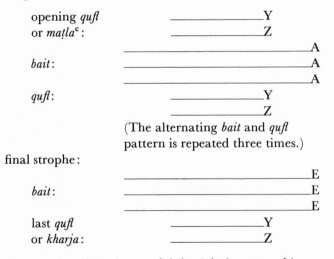

		____________W
qufl:		____________X
		____________Y
		____________Z

(The alternating *bait* and *qufl* pattern is repeated three times.)

final strophe:

	____________I	____________J
	____________I	____________J
bait:	____________I	____________J
	____________I	____________J
	____________I	____________J

		____________W
last *qufl*		____________X
or *kharja*:		____________Y
		____________Z

Many different combinations are possible, of course; and it seems that the more complex the *muwashshaḥ* is, the later it was written. A more lyrical simplicity apparently preceded technical virtuosity.

The last *qufl* in a *muwashshaḥ* is called a *kharja*, which means "exit." This differs from the rest of the poem in that it is supposed to be written without classical Arabic's desinential inflection, which must be present in all other parts of the poem. Only in a panegyric *muwashshaḥ*, when the name of the person being praised is mentioned in the *kharja*, may the formal grammatical inflections be maintained, for example. Ibn Sanā' al-Mulk explains that other exceptions to this rule occur when the *kharja* is forceful and passionate, representing conversation between lovers, when it is as jolting and fascinating as a sorceress, or if it contains a quotation from a classical poem. Such exceptions, nevertheless, are rare. The *kharja* may be composed in a foreign language, in colloquial Arabic, or in a regional dialect, not a phrase of which would be acceptable in the main body of the poem, where classical Arabic prevails. This is just one of the *kharja*'s ways of adding spice to the *muwashshaḥ*. Although the *kharja* is situated at the end of the poem, it is paradoxically the beginning, he reveals. This is due to the fact that the *kharja* is supposed to come into the poet's mind first. It is the cornerstone on which he builds the rest of the *muwashshaḥ*, the model according to which he constructs the rhyme and meter of the other *qufls* and with which he must blend each *bait*.

The introduction to the *kharja*, which occurs in the last *bait*, should be abrupt, furnishing a quick change of pace, and should indicate who the speaker is. The speaker, who fits into various categories, may be a man or a woman, a drunkard, a bird, or even a city. In addition, the final stanza should include an introductory verb like "he said" or "she sang" before giving the direct speech of the *kharja*. When it comes to using another person's words, colloquial or foreign dialects are permissible. Famous lines of another poet may also be borrowed and turned into the *kharja*, or the *kharja* itself may be taken from another *muwashshaḥ*.[5] Ibn Sanā' al-Mulk says that this procedure is better than composing a bad *kharja*. Although this opinion is valid, it is limited in its point of view. García Gómez, explaining that Ibn Sanā' al-Mulk was writing descriptively and without historical perspective, interprets this borrowing as an indication that the first *kharjas* were taken from elsewhere, possibly from a popular or traditional source.[6] One should keep in mind the fact that Ibn Sanā' al-Mulk could not read or understand the Romance dialect of Spain and consequently was hampered in his appraisal of the situation.

His lack of familiarity with the Romance culture of al-Andalus also prevented him from understanding the metrics of most *muwashshaḥs*. Although he is able to measure the few poems which fall into the categories of classical Arabic meter,[7] he is at a loss to explain the majority of *muwashshaḥs* which can not be scanned in accordance with Arabic metrics. His only recourse is to music, for these lyrics were meant to be sung. He believes that they have no other meter except that of their musical arrangement and that, by hearing them sung, one can distinguish adequate *muwashshaḥs* from the lame ones. Since none of the music has survived, it would be difficult to judge how satisfactory this method proved to be. Contemporary efforts to understand this problem have produced an alternative explanation, however. García Gómez has formulated the hypothesis that by applying the principle of Romance syllabic count to *muwashshaḥs* which seem amorphous to Arabic-speaking critics, the riddle of their structure could be solved. Poems which strike Ibn Sanā' al-Mulk as being very strange can easily be analyzed in terms of syllables, García Gómez posits.[8] He has also demonstrated that Mussafia's law, which counts an accented syllable at the end of a line as one syllable rather than two, can be applied to strophic Arabic poetry written in al-Andalus.[9] Poets living in the bilingual Andalusian environment might have taken such an indigenous system for granted if it was an inherent part of the poetry and song to which they were exposed.[10]

Ibn Sanā' al-Mulk is on firmer ground when he discusses thematic material. He points out that the same topics found in classical Arabic poetry are developed in the *muwashshaḥs*: erotic, ascetic, panegyric, and satyrical. In doing this, Ibn Sanā' al-Mulk was not trying to establish a fixed law. He was merely observing the general qualities of the *muwashshaḥs* he knew, and his description appears to be accurate. The one aspect which he could not be expected to consider was the thematic content of the Mozarabic *kharjas*, written in a language he did not comprehend. These bilingual poems will be considered in the second part of this book, and I hope that some long-standing questions concerning the difference between the Arabic *muwashshaḥs* and those with Mozarabic *kharjas* may then be answered.

CHAPTER TWO
Translation: An Andalusian Anthology in *The House of Embroidery* (*Dār al-Ṭirāz*)

The second part of Ibn Sanā' al-Mulk's treatise consists of an anthology of Andalusian *muwashshaḥs* that were written totally in Arabic. Not only do these *muwashshaḥs* serve as illustrations for his theory, but they also comprise one of the very few collections extant. In regard to the varied examples of formal structure, it presents a well-organized, complete picture. Ibn Sanā' al-Mulk begins with the simplest prosodic construction and, poem by poem, works his way through to the most complex, choosing what he considers to be the best *muwashshaḥ* in each category. Since he collected these examples himself, none could have been composed after 1211, the year of his death. Most of the *muwashshaḥs* were probably composed during the twelfth century, although the poems by Ibn al-Labbāna and Ibn ᶜUbāda date back to the eleventh century, along with some of the anonymous ones. Many questions about this anthology remain unanswered. Where problems of historical period and authorship are concerned, however, I have accepted García Gómez's experienced judgment.

When translating these poems, I was working with an unvoweled text, which is a difficult task. Needless to say, I am acutely aware of inaccuracies and ambiguities which have yet to be resolved. Nevertheless, I believe that these *muwashshaḥs* are sufficiently lovely and valuable to warrant the effort. Although nothing can ever replace the lyrical quality of the Arabic poems, I hope that the English translation of this anthology will give an accurate impression of the original metaphors and images. In order to be as faithful as possible to the Arabic text, I have not forced the English into stiff molds of rhyme or meter. The musical quality of the verse must be heard in Arabic to be appreciated. English sounds cannot duplicate it, and attempts at imitation would only have warped the meaning.

Many *muwashshaḥs* may strike the Western ear as strange and unusual. With hardly any transition at all, the poets jump from one theme to another and back again. To one whose ear is accustomed to more gradual transitions and a better balance between form and content, the Arabic style can be quite disconcerting at first; but by immersing oneself in the *muwashshaḥs* long enough to adjust to new rhythms and patterns, one can emerge with a fresh appreciation of this ornate and expressive style.

I

By al-Aᶜmā al-Tuṭīlī

When he laughs he reveals pearls.
When unveiled a full moon appears.
Time is too narrow to hold him,
Yet he is contained within my heart.

Woe unto me for what I suffer! My afflictions make me so thin that people can see through me.
He is so inconsistent with me,[1] sometimes violent, other times slow and deliberate.
Whenever I said, "Enough!" he would say to me, "How can you be so sure?"

He moves like the bough of a weeping willow,
The possessor of fresh green movement
With which dally the hands
Of the wind and the rain.

I must have you. Take my heart, humbly given.
I have no patience left but nonetheless will keep on striving.
You're like a spring of honey, and my longing for you testifies.

How can the daughter of earthen vessels
Be compared to that mouth?
What is the strength of wine
In contrast to the face of time?

I have a hidden love. If only my efforts would succeed!
Whenever it appears, it is contained within the horizon of my heart.
The passion arising from this vision cannot be cured.

By my father, how did
A bright celestial sphere
Become so clear that it made evident
His excuse and my plea?[2]

Is there any way to reach you? Or must I give up all hope?
I have all but wasted away from weeping and sighing.
What should I say? I get suspicious when I hear, "Perhaps."
Everything was decided
While I was zealously persisting,
Releasing the reins
Of my anxiety and forbearance.

How would it hurt the one who blames me if he were to leave me alone?
Have I done anything wrong except to love a white antelope whose religion is to incriminate others?
I am passionately in love with him. And he sings to me,
"I have seen that you are ailing.
What's wrong with you?[3] You know
Time will pass
And you will forget me."

2

From the Almoravid period, probably by al-Aᶜmā al-Tuṭīlī

The severity of the lover is sweeter than the honey of bees.
The sorrowful one must accept humiliation.
I am at war with the glances of the wide-eyed one.
I cannot cope with seductive jet-black eyes.
Whoever sees his eyelids will ruin his religion.

Oppression from ones like you is unavoidable for men.
If you would give in to me, then I would be as proud as the sun.
Goal of my desire, come, be sociable!
You are my festival and your cheek is my garden.
Cover the jasmine, lest men pluck it.

The vizier maps out his chosen plans,
But the joys end in a different way.
Things returned to a fierce lion
Who is firm of heart, turning away from the delinquent one.
He guarded his lair with sharpened spears.

Let every lie be followed by truth.
Has anyone ever seen with his own eyes one who obtained supreme authority
Like Abū al-Ḥusayn? What generous one is willing to ransom him?
Everyone who deserves gratitude, even all the falling rain,
Wishing to be like him in generosity, falls short.

The one who is living in exile has suffered deprivation.
And I am blamed if I conceal or declare my feelings.
I said, and the words will make it clear this time,
"I obtained what I desired when he was generous with gifts.
May God uphold the establishment of the magistrate of the city."

3

By Ḥātim ibn Saᶜīd

As the sun goes hand in hand with a full moon,
So wine is accompanied by a drinking companion.
Pass around the cups of wine perfumed with ambergris. The garden has become joyful
And the wafting breeze
Has clothed the river with a coat of mail.

The hand of the East and the West[4] has pulled out lightninglike swords on the horizon,
And weeping clouds
Have made the flowers laugh.

Behold! I have a lord who has dominated, has made himself master. Except for
My tears, which uncovered the secret,
I would have been discreet.

How do you expect me to maintain secrecy while my tears are causing a flood in which fires are blazing?
For who has seen live embers
Floating on a fathomless sea?

When someone who saw his unfairness blamed me for my love, I sang this melody:
"Perhaps he has an excuse
While you are blaming."

4
Anonymous

The hand of the rain untied the buds of the
  blossoms. So, oh, my friend, drink!

Drink! The morning draught is good today.
In a fragrant meadow, in the presence of clouds,
She rose, appearing before the people,
  While the face of that day was eclipsed by a veil
    of darkness.

You were unjust when you stayed away from the one who loved you.
So return to where you were, close to me.
You deceived me and bolted, oh, my darling.
  I am ready to ransom you even if you are a faithless one,
  faithful only to flight, and are not near.

This passion tyrannizes, so what can I do?
I can not control it, oh, Manṣūr.
I have no help except my tears.
  Oh, how weak my victory over sorrow would be as long as
    my tears are my only support.

Beloved, give your consent and take my life.
Let me drink again from the deep red lips of your mouth,
Together with the kind of witchcraft your eyes contain.
  Cool my burning fire and sheath the swordlike glances.
    Don't kill me!

When he prolonged my grief and had no mercy,
And his aggression increased and he did not consent,
I began to sing the song of an enamored one, which I sing now:
  "My darling, you are my neighbor. Your house is next
    to mine, yet you are avoiding me."

5
From the Almoravid period, probably by Ibn Baqī or al-Aᶜmā al-Tuṭīlī

Pass us the drinking glass to help us forget the
  passion of love,
And summon the companions, as friendship requires.

Submit to desire like a law as long as you live, oh, my friend.
Don't listen to the speech of one who blames you,
For it is a rule that wine should be brought to you by one with

Fingertips of jujube and candied fruit of the rose,
Bordered by two locks of myrtle which curve around
the cheek.

How magnificent were the days in which the wine circulated
And the meadow was smiling where rain had fallen early,
When reunion and familiarity and faces were like flowers.
We were with friends, strung together like a necklace.
Oh, Abū ᶜAbbās, may good luck not betray you.

Your Caliph among us is Abū Bakr.
He represents you in prohibiting and commanding for us.
We do not have to protect ourselves against poverty brought by the
turns of fate.
You are lords of what glory has constructed,
And if we were to test all men, then they would
contrast sharply with you.

The world became adorned after having been bare
When Yaḥyā came to us among the venerable lords,
Dazzling in his exaltedness upon a white-footed steed.
He swaggers in robes which praise has embroidered
And his friendship overflows. For him there are
no limits.

While I was drinking a pure beverage,
I was repenting, but still wavering,
When a friend from the group of aesthetes said to me,
"Our companion has repented. Sing and serenade him!
Present him with the drinking cup. Perhaps he
will relapse."

6
Anonymous

Oh, stingy one to whom I am generous despite my
poverty and need,
I love you, and in addition to that I have my
longing and remembrance.

Aren't you ashamed of procrastinating while I have been complaining for
such a long time?
And why isn't reunion with you nearer to the one who seeks it?
Where has your dream-shadow disappeared since my tears have flowed like
rain clouds for it?

And don't say, "Perhaps it has gone astray during
these travels."[5]
Your memory has kindled fire from a stone out of love
and thirst for you.

I suffer because of longing, but will not reveal it.
If silence is a *topos*, then I have spoken eloquently.
Oh, one who commits a crime and accuses me, I have a complaint.
If only it could do some good!
Come! But I do not think you will do so. My
patience has been lost.
Watch out for a complaint which, if repeated,
would kindle fire with fire.

What's the use of yearning, which makes the eye shed tears and fills
the heart with ardor?
How can you see my illness and still pretend ignorance of my love?
Ask about me: "Who has made me forget my name and who has trespassed
against my heart?"
But if you ask, do not trust those who envy the
celestial flowers.
Your eyes are more worthy to witness and are
better informed about what I hide.

My master, Abū al-ᶜAlā', if you permit me to speak
And I don't allude to rejection except to make beauty flourish,
Is there separation or union after the swiftness of praise?
Suppose I stay while you depart. Fate has many
hazards.
Consumed with grief over you, who could sleep[6] in
the straits of anguished captivity?

Hoping for an encounter, I roamed about those quarters,
Making rounds which are not permitted, while tears veiled my face.
So sing about coquetry and send a message about humility:
"By God, oh, pampered bird brought up in the
desert,
Take care not to persist in your habit of
throwing stones in my house!"

7
Anonymous

Skeletal traces of the encampment revive
my sorrow. Is it possible
To find solace for my longing heart?
Die, oh, consolation!

Oh, vestige which predestined my death,
You were thirsty. Here are the tears of my eye
Which pour forth, so quench your thirst at the fountain.[7]
But, oh, you who have departed, you are to blame for
my sin. Perhaps the time has come
For me to die. Then woe! Alas!

Oh, territory of love, are you about to kill me?
This passion is increasing.
Separation came to you right after he turned away.
Oh, one tested by all grave affairs, how long are
you going to be sad? How long will you mourn
And be troubled about a love whose passion wanes and
is forgetful?

My censurers, I don't want to forget him.
I am suffering because of a white antelope on a hill.
The mention of his name is sweet to my heart.
But mentioning the name of every beautiful thing is my
occupation, which consoles and does me good,
Whereas the core of my heart neglects everyone but him.

How often does the ghost of fantasy make me desire
While preventing a true reunion!
If only he could hear me complain about my condition.
But he will never pity the one in love, whether he
conceals or reveals it.
How many lovers would go astray if he called them?

How often was he my drinking companion!
His mouth with well-arranged pearls is my candied fruit,
And whenever he says, "Yes," my paradise comes closer.
It is all just a game with me, yet I am satisfied with
dark red lips which, when he smiles,
Reveal sweet food that is delicious. I sip from his
radiant mouth.

I said while death was heading straight for me,
When he said, "Tomorrow I must go,"
And stretched out his hand to me in farewell,
"I commend to the Lord's protection the one to whom
I say farewell, and I ask God
To make my heart patient while he is away. Alas!"

8

From the court of al-Muᶜtamid, possibly by Ibn al-Labbāna

One who is madly in love spends the evening
looking at the stars.
He finds the pain sweet and is delighted with
his states of grief and anxiety.

Those with large black eyes have given the soul a cup of nectar to
drink.
The pupils of their eyes are surrounded by nothing but pretty gardens
made of
Cheeks which have been chipped from lilies and red anemones.
Under the luminous forehead, myrtle on a downy
cheek is bent to foretell
That water of the mouth,[8] around which it circles,
is going from me.

I wish that there had been no day of separation from the one who made
me dress in a robe of grief,
When the gazelle of our quarter twisted my patience as he gazed there
And thought that passion was a sin. He therefore was stingy with what
I desired.
The miserly one has destroyed the light of my patience
in the darkness of my weeping,
And for fear of punishment, my heart begged for sympathy
and then confessed the sin.

He scared slumber away from me and I spent the night complaining about
what I suffer
To the horses which you see whose backs are quickly carrying me.
I did not praise night travel until I beheld al-Muᶜtamid.
In him I saw the coexistence of worldly and religious
things. We are matching him against those who
preceded, and he exceeds them.
Whoever finds fault with him is looking at something
good behind a veil.

His victory is assured by the sharp-edged spear.
He is as generous to his generation as rain clouds are to gardens.[9]
It's as if the mention of his name were a Koranic verse to be recited to all mankind.

> His two states consist of strength and tenderness. So say, "Beware if he stands for war!"
> And say that the clouds, if they open their palms, do not release terror.

And the good bird alighted at my house at sunset.
Around the net of cunning he picks up kernels of hearts.
As soon as he descended he flew away, so here is a song of the sad one:

> "If only you could have seen what kind of a bird alighted at my house and stopped beside me!
> When he saw the trap, he balanced his wings and departed with my heart."

9
By Ibn ᶜUbāda

> I'm ready to give my father as ransom for a precious one who is attached to my soul.

I loved a new moon, incomparable in its beauty. The eyes and long lovely neck of the gazelle are modeled after it.[10]
He swaggered in his beauty, which desires no increase,[11] a full moon shining in perfect proportion.

> Elegance adorned him and his figure was slender.

He is a full moon that triumphs with sheer magic. The down on his cheek is curved over jasmine.
A lily was placed beside a well-guarded rose whenever he came into view, trailing his beautiful train behind.[12]

> He appeared to me as a creature worthy of excessive passion.

My eyes live just to attend him. If only my soul had feathers, I would fly to him.
Beauty has made his eyes like swords[13] and his glances are arrows feathered with legitimate magic.[14]

> He has a slender shape, and the heart is aroused by desire.

He intended to leave me when I yielded to love, and I squandered my
patience in spite of his prolonged rejection.
Water of beauty moves on the page of his cheek. His teeth put to shame
the symmetry of a pearl.
His mouth is a delicate box, worthy of a kiss.

When he cloaked himself in a stylish robe, I wanted to kiss his delicious
red lips.
So he spoke in verse, playing the role of one who refuses, and coyly
inclined with the sweetest expression:
"I say, by God, you will never taste the sugarplum!"[15]

10

Probably by Ibn Baqī

Have you been unique in your beauty or was
your creation unique?

I see you have a sharp lance of Indian iron, surrounded by antimony,
and so it unsheathed what can not be described.[16]
Oh, one with enchanting eyelids, your sword
is very keen.

Oh, temptation of the heart, fear God in regard to the lover who
has been killed by passion.
You promise to give rain clouds, but your lightning
is deceptive.

When is a debt, which this separation imposed, going to be paid?
Your eyes are on me,
So my eyes and ears will never turn away.

Your mounts are saddled and start earnestly on their journey. I
greeted you, but you did not reply,
Even though you knew I was alarmed by the separation.

I encountered unbounded grief because of the distance, so I said out
of love,
"My beloved has left me. When will I be with him again?"

11

By Ibn al-Labbāna

How long will the one whose eyes are languid
yet healthy, not smitten by sleeplessness,
keep me awake?

My tears have revealed what I would conceal and my heart yearns for the one who treats it unjustly,
A gazelle whose mouth is used to saying, "No." How often do I desire to kiss it!
It reveals well-ordered pearls. How nice it would be if daisies had such fragrant breath.

Is there any way to drink the kisses? How far I am from attaining that hope!
Before accomplishing that, one must face eyes like swords which unsheath glances, both brazen and bashful.
He showed us something red amid the white: the cheek of morning with a glow of twilight in it.

Who will enable me to do justice in praising the Banū ᶜAbbād and thanking them adequately?
Those gifts which they gave me were very unexpected. I forgive the one who envies me because of them.
Doves resemble me among the leaves. The Banū ᶜAbbād provided my wings with feathers. Then they put a ring around my neck.[17]

How magnificent is a king of Yaᶜrub who has relied on God![18] He is the most noble of them in liberality.
And they pour forth like seas and roar like a lion if an embassy appears.
If they are assailed or summoned, equally they hasten forth with wine and a vessel of milk out of generosity.

Time has been good to us and moderate as long as we have had this dynasty, which has made us heirs of joy.
It brought back words of youth and love, so I said when my beloved left,
"Send the greeting with the wind for an anxious lover who does not trust mankind."

12

By Ibn al-Labbāna

Thus the light of the shining stars[19] leads the way
To the seated ones when water is mixed with wine in the glasses.

Accept my excuse, for it is time to devote oneself to
Wine, which is passed around by one who has luxuriant eyebrows.
As you know, he is slender and lean.
    Whenever he moves in the meadow of garments,
    You see myrtle with its leaves swaying to and fro.

He is human even though he is more radiant
Than the sun and the full moon on a dark night.
My soul belongs to him and is not forsaken.
    He is a gazelle who hunted the strongest lions
    With harsh glances which penetrate people's homes.

Let me leave alone the subject of rejection and flight.
Take from me the two reports concerning glory
And say that I am going to talk about the sea.[20]
    Rashīd of the Banū ᶜAbbād was victorious and generous
    And he has made men forget Rashīd of the Banū ᶜAbbās.[21]

His image dispelled darkness by the light of true religion
And so the stars strive to reach his height.
Thus kings are servants of ᶜUbaid Allāh.
    So whoever wished to compare you to another in matters of glory
    Compared in ignorance the light of the sun to a lantern.

Nobility is yours and you are from a noble family.
All see the attainment of favours they hope for through you,
So the one who sings does not leave in his former condition.
    "Banū ᶜAbbād, because of you we are enjoying festivals
    And weddings. May you live forever for the people's sake!"

13

Anonymous, but possibly by Ibn al-Labbāna

He who has charged the eyes with cutting swords of Indian metal
And has made sweet basil grow on the side of his cheek
Has inflicted tears and sleeplessness upon the one who is madly in love.
Is there any way to keep silent
    For the lover burdened with tears which reveal, as they flow forth, the secret he hides
    Concerning one who wears no jewels, yet is adorned, who is outwardly naive and overpowers me with large black eyes?

Oh, I'd give my father as ransom for a black-eyed one who is like
the full moon.
He reveals a gem whose kiss is delightful.
His flowerlike cheek blushes at just a thought,
So how can I be absolved?
A speckled serpent crept over the brazilwood,
so don't kiss it!
By magic he appointed an army of Ethiopians,
together with Nabateans, to kill heroes.

The time has come to emanate light, like the lord of the mountain,
Like a full moon in darkness, with a body as slim as a reed,
Like a branch of beryl in a rounded hillock of camphor.
By the soul of an abandoned one
I ransom him, even though it makes me an orphan.
In a sealed place are the teeth of his mouth,
and they have been set in order
Like pearls on strings, with perfumed spaces between,
providing my wine and my cool water.

Just as you have been endowed with beauty, oh, Aḥmad,
So is command devoted to you, oh, delicate one.
Your slave is in love with you and subjugated.
Are you going to reprimand me?
Or will you have mercy and prevent the wasting away of
the one in love if he becomes ill with grief?
Woe unto me! I am imprisoned in a sea of fears whose
shore is far away. I can only cling to the waves.

Sometimes a young girl appears like the full moon rising.
What a breast on a branch of laurel!
Her leaves are a garment more red than the rose.
She spent the night while singing,
"My darling, make up your mind. Arise! Hurry and
kiss my mouth. Come embrace
My breast and raise my anklets to my earrings. My
husband is busy."

14
Probably by al-Aᶜmā al-Tuṭīlī or Ibn Baqī

I would give my father in ransom for this red-lipped
slim one who does not pity when it comes to love.
May God treat with justice the one who loves passionately
in the face of rejection.

No one contains all the charms of the time except a gazelle
Who is of noble blood. A maternal and paternal uncle are from Fihr.
This kinship is like being related to lavish generosity and courage.
I love him because of glory and beauties.
His face is bright and open, shining for the guests,
And his hand controls the lion that is terrified.

He has such outstanding qualities that it is difficult to describe, so call him a knight or a handsome one.
He leans towards generosity, swaying to and fro in every breeze.
Tell me, since my thoughts are but vain ones,
How the fawn returning to its covert became a wary lion.
He rides a noble thoroughbred, which no one can overtake.
His mind concentrates on hunting and glory.

Because Ibn Ṣaddīn Abū al-Walīd turned away, I
Am like hunted quarry which has just been cut through the jugular vein.
He went forth in the morning with hounds wagging their tails and running. There is no escape.
The hounds attach themselves firmly to what they are after.
They begin to circle around him, like arrows which have been shot,
Not following a path in lowland or highland.

If only you could have seen a tyrant rejoicing as a free man does
When the attacking animal hit the hare hard in the vital part of its body
And bloody death was dripping from its claws and ankle,
And when they took its heart and fled without turning back.
Hurrying like lightning over them is the sparrow hawk
Whose wings in flight are like thunder clapping.

Therefore marvel at him as he swaggers when he moves.
He silenced poets with the inimitability of his description.
You only see him passing quickly by on his purebred horse.
Beauty gave a robe of honor to the falcon on his wrist.
His creation was a strong one. His plumage is silk embroidered with gold,
Which he wrapped as a cloak that will never wear out.

Oh, one who asks the lover about his illness, do not ask.
Truly the one I adored was not fair in his judgment.
In regard to the hunt, he acts according to the old tricks.
If only my anxiety were his worry when it was said to me,

"The gazelle crosses the plain and the greyhounds
hasten behind.
My sadness is nothing but guilty intentions which
almost succeeded, but they did not overtake him."

15
By Ibn ᶜUbāda

Under the umbrella of the weeping willow, hidden
beneath its branches, how many moon-faced
and long-necked ones
With finger tips and joints painted with red henna
presented themselves to a receiver.

They are wild gazelles that hunt the lion.
They have no covert except the hearts of the bewildered.
Being near them is a wedding; being far from them is a funeral.
Those dark red lips give life to the one who longs for them.
They have languid glances which gaze at the one who has become
emaciated.
With the eyes of gazelles they smile, revealing jewels
arranged on the thread of a necklace.
The jealous one decreed that they be hidden in the
heart of hearts.

I love a gazelle. Loving him is bewitching me. What a killer he is!
His glances have made my heart like a frightened bird,
And the heart did not stop being bewildered about love as long as he
made it sick.
When he became strong, he became less just.
Oh, unjust judge, you wrong one who does not commit any crime at all.
Fear the authority of the Merciful One when he judges
between the innocent and the sinners.
You wrongly attacked the one in love, and he did not
ask for assistance, oh, attacker.

Woe unto the one who desires the beloved who has forgotten.
It is unjustly decreed that the one smitten with dearth should be
drowned in tears
And that his suffering heart should shake
As if it were an ornament hung upon those necks.
So I said, questioning, "Who made
My heart throb?" So he said, 'Stand and perceive on
the shore
The banners of the ships of war and seek information
from the pendants."

Don't you see them standing high upon a spear, fluttering
On skiffs which move like race horses ahead of all others?
They were constructed by the one who produces the rain-yielding cloud
in a season of drought,
Masts higher than the stars with limbs that are lofty.
Verily the Pleiades say, and they tell the truth,
"There is no place above this in terms of ambition
which can vie in height with him.
His foot is higher than Saturn. Jupiter is lower
than he."

Stars of the kingdom are shining, a source of good fortune for the
Muslims,
Penetrating the darkness and leading to victory and success.
After the warning of the stars, the morning of those who are warned
will turn out badly.
They sing in praise of the emir as far as the towns of the Christians.
Wherever he directs himself, they fly as quickly as a wink.
The smile of lances has been set in order like the
teeth of combs,
And the sea is like a volcano burning with the frenzy
of something soaked in oil.

How many festivals he has! Each one is a day that is lovely to view.
He is a sea whose sand resembles all good amber.
Muḥammad and his army have occupied the shore.
His foot rides the ship which resembles a slender horse.
So a servant of his said, finding pleasant what he saw,
"What a wonderful festival this is! The sand effuses
a fragrance like amber for the one who walks
While the ships are like eagles and al-Muʿtaṣim is
with his army on the shore."

16

Anonymous

Come early for wine and smell the flowers!
Life is worthless as long as there is no intoxication.
Seldom do I forgo sipping from the drinking cups
While a bewitching glance is helping at the social
gathering.
So give me the daughter of the vine to drink!

Bring it in pure form, oh, gazelle with large black eyes—
Wine which resembles a description of your moonlit cheek.

He is a gazelle that represents nobility and justice
among men
And musk where perfume from his fragrant breath is
concerned.
Protect me from the musk of Dārīn!

How many rascals have blamed me about him
When they saw a tendency in him to respond to me.
But despite the blame, for there is no wrong in it,
His saliva cures one of sickness and increases
sociability.
Congratulate me! I am not among those who have been
deceived.

A careless glance will bring painful results
As long as the power of kingship is in Sulayma's power.
Everyone reveres him. He is a supple spear shaft,
swaying to and fro,
Bending to form a curve like a branch of myrtle
Because of its suppleness—so soft it could
easily be cut into shreds.

By God, how lovely is the young girl who sings to him,
Willfully revealing the complaint in order to trouble him with it:
"You are the desire which is sweet, so leave the
conversation of people
And enter with me, my love, like wine in a cup,
Oh, Kannūnī, in order to cheer me up."

17
Possibly by Ibn Baqī

The sleepless hostage of anxiety rendered useless
all efforts of the visitors.[22]
Love humiliated him, but one who loves passionately
does not mind submissiveness.

How nice it would be for me if he would gaze with the eyes of an
enchanter at the worshipers.
Beauty keeps him at a distance and, bolting, he turns away, difficult
to lead.
Sometimes he comes near, like a bird sipping water from a
pool.[23]

His neck is soft and slim, and his cheek is adorned
by a mole.
Veils hide it and I have a desire for the veil.

When he raised his neck and passed by like a gazelle in the
wilderness,
The jingling ornaments around his neck indicated where he was.
The languidness of his eyes hastens the convalescence of one who is
sick from loving him.
If I ask him for anything, then woe unto me if he
glances.
Is the heart safe while arrows of his glance are
aimed at it?

I wish that my dear friend—and in his mouth is the sweet bouquet of
the wine glass—
Would grant me a reunion as generously as Abū ʿAbbās bestows his
wealth.
He is the possessor of glory and virtue. Say, "He is superior to
other men in rank."
Oh, one towards whom all lordship is turned, even
with wealth you are not concerned.
You are like a quick horse who competes and outstrips
all others.

Oh, you who are thirsty, do you have any fresh water which fills
buckets?
Then seek the Banū Q̄āsim, and go from the west to Salé,
And urge on the camels which tread heavily as they move proudly
through the desert
Like ships that struggle in the seas of mirage and
are not drowned.
The riders rejoice while the she-camels complain of
the journey.

I call him judge, and my hope judges that he will rule in my favor.
I am satisfied with him because he is going to fulfill my wish.
Say: "There is no substitute for him among those who dwell on earth."
Say:
"Don't you see that Aḥmad can not be surpassed in
his great glory?
The West gave rise to him. So show us the likes
of him, oh, East!"

18
Probably by Ibn ʿUbāda

By my father I'd ransom an inaccessible gazelle who is guarded by lions of the thicket.
My doctrine consists of sipping from the dark red lips whose wine is from the spring of Salsabīl.[24]
He captures my heart with his slim body which bends when he moves.
He possesses symmetry and traces his origin to one who has the beneficence of Thābit.
He spends the night in the shade under pleasant dew drops.

He has languid eyes, a flirtatious way of speaking, and red lips.
He is all perfumes in one, when it comes to sweet aromas, and beauty itself in dress.
How much passion he arouses in the grieving one, clothed in a long illness.
The langorous one, if he would give but a drink, could make the mute speak.
A gazelle, if he but cast a glance, could restore the vision of the dazzled.

To find the limit of this brilliant one is to discover the limit of passion.
To seek his watering place is to seek the water of the river Kauthar,[25] the secret of thirst.
Look at Muḥammad and linger with him.
He is like a crescent moon beyond description when revealed.
He is cool, pure water. If given generously, it bewitches even the pious.

He is a full moon, a sun of early morning, a branch on a sand dune, redolent musk.
How full! How bright! How rich in leaves! How aromatic!
Indeed the one who glances at him has loved passionately and has been deprived.
So reunion was but a fleeting hope which passed,
And the vision was something which arose from a dying breath.

My murderer, spare the blood of one who became a heretic.
My companion you once were. What turned you away from that which had seemed good?
My inquisitor who asks, the army of destruction has been brutal.

There is no point in asking about an anguished
man, who has wasted away in silence
So that he might be given what he hoped for,
as long as the matter is in the hands
of a sadist.

How haughty he is! How much so! And how stubbornly passion refuses to change!
I am content with him even though he decreed that desire should rule over reason.
I said about him, and love is only pleased with what I say,
"Beauty is an endowment bestowed upon the gazelle
of the Banū Thābit.
In love there is no end, no, to the steadfast covenant
made with him."

19

By Ibn Baqī

The most amazing thing is that I remain
faithful
To one who refuses to be loyal to me and
who wishes my death.

What was done was done for the love of beauty.
The one enslaved by passion is not like one who is sober.
Don't you see that healthy people are freer than those who are sick?
Arrows have been notched and aimed for a death that was predetermined.
Oh, you who are killing me by shooting these
arrows,
Grant me a meeting, if only in a dream.

Don't blame me, for the affair is serious.
A gazelle who looked at me has captured my faith.
He was adorned by beauty among the black-eyed ones.
Nothing can cure me of my love except
The red lips and two well-arranged strands of
a necklace
That mix honey with pure wine.

Leader of the caravan, make our mounts hurry
Toward the one who captures the heart of the free,
Or else turn me toward Ibn ᶜAlī,
The possessor of overflowing generosity and brilliant judgment.

If he appears, say: "Oh, perfect crescent
moon."
Or if the rain is far away, then he is the
rain cloud which floods the earth.

How could he not be there, assuming that the time is favorable.
He is a unique star which clothes me with light.
Praise speaks about him with its tongue.
He and glory are foster brothers who shared the same milk.
How often he has felt ashamed of those who carry
out ignoble acts.
May he live forever in exaltedness.

Fate has decreed that you be unique
And that your majesty be singular. Your excellence is evidence.
And when it comes to mentioning the most noble ones,
Glory recites about these sights,
"Truly Yaḥyā is the scion of noble lineage,
Unique in the world, and the quintessence
of mankind."

20
By Ibn Baqī

I have no wine but sorrow.
Mixing with it in the cup are tears
which flow continuously.

How abundant are the tears that have been scattered
By an amorous man who cried because of an ardent love.
A wild fawn killed him on the day of battle.[26]
He has been killed—no, rather wounded by
a lance.
Hovering between hope and despair, death
awaits him.

I have been wounded to the point of death and can only wring my hands.
Something came between me and my friend.
There is no doubt that separation is causing my death.
The time for departure came while there were
debts still due me.
If al-ᶜAbbās were to disclaim them, then he
would be like al-Amīn.[27]

Don't you see the full moon? The moon of good fortune
Has dressed in green striped garments.
When he bends with fresh radiance among the other figures,
He begins to say, "Die, oh, sorrowful one.
The jasmine has been clad with myrtle."

I said, when he had driven sleep away from me
And deprived the visitors of all hope because of my disease,
"Go away from me!" And when he went, I gnashed my teeth.
My body is so emaciated that one can hardly see it.
Companions look for it where the moan is.

My heart has exceeded its limit in longing
And has left me sleepless. If only I could bear it!
I said, while night extended a tent around me,
"What a long night without a single helper!
Oh, heart of someone, can't you be assuaged?"

21

By Ibn ᶜUbāda

Let me look at the lightning which has
frozen like pearls.[28]
In it there are hailstones which have been
set in order, and so it is adorned.

On the day of parting, in the place of separation,
Desire offered me two opposites—
Fire of passion and tears of the eye.
So my sorrows catch fire and burn fiercely,
While my eyes overflow continuously with tears.

Say to the enemies: "The religion of right guidance
Has drawn its two swords through the resolution of its two kings
And has strengthened the affection of its two lovers."
This is a union which has been sealed,
a rope which has been tied, a structure
Which will never be demolished. Its pillars are
everlasting.

Abū Yaḥyā has united with Abū al-Qāsim,
So the source of water has given great pleasure to the thirsty one
And the way of escape has become narrow for the oppressor.
They are two bountiful seas for those who
came to them thirsty.
They are two swords of vengeance for anyone
who is disloyal.

Has anyone else created such glory,
Or has anyone beside these two clothed himself with praise?
They are two full moons of the highest sphere which have not
lacked good fortune.
They possess so much wisdom that it would tire
the mind of Lokman.[29]
In aspirations, they go beyond the sphere of Saturn.

All mankind takes that into account.
Among noble men, both are unique.
Truly doves in their forest sing,
"Say, have there ever been known or experienced
or have there been
Two rulers like al-Mu^{c}taṣim and al-Mu^{c}taḍid?"

22

Possibly by Ibn Baqī or al-A^{c}mā al-Tuṭīlī

The palpitations of my heart are excessive
and my patience is gone.
My love has let me go. If only I could
let go of him!

Who could mean as much to me as this slender one who disturbs the mind?
He gazes through thick eyebrows, like burnished cutting swords.
He moves his body like a branch covered with dew.
As the south wind blew when he ambled, I
said,
"If I were to sell my heart for his love,
I would profit."

Allow my eyes to wander through the garden of your cheeks.
These are my debts which have dwindled in your presence.
I am satisfied with my death if it is from your hand,
Oh, one who is all goodness. Beauty is an
attribute of his.
What kind of a sin is it to love the one I
love?

Oh, one who accuses me falsely, may you not taste what I have—
A troubled heart and freely flowing tears.
May I be your ransom, branch. My love for him is natural.
He is a branch of the dune, supple when it
bends. I have grown old.
My time has run out since he and I were
separated from one another.[30]

Beauty knows that you are even more beautiful than he.
You are more noble, and death has no power over you.
The enamored one ransoms you. He keeps a secret until it
 becomes evident.
  You are my share of all that I proposed.
  It is enough. What you wish is enough for me,
   not what I wish.

You and I share this separation.
Stoically, you left at the break of dawn,
And since you have gone, the passion in my heart has sung,
  "My beloved left at dawn and I did not
   say farewell to him.
  Oh, lonely heart of mine at night when I
   remember him!"

23
By Ibn ᶜUbāda

  Go for the wine! And go early with an embroidered
   robe
  In the evening and the morning to the music of the
   eloquent bowstring.

The name of wine, in my opinion—so know it!—is not taken from anything
 but
The one who is *khā*' of the cheek and *mīm* of the smile
And *rā*' of the honeyed saliva from a fragrant mouth.[31]
  Give up worrying and join these letters
  So that you might go early and late with a
   body that has spirit.

By God, give me a drink of it, for the love of Wāthiq,
For truly he has similar qualities to those found in wine.
He who has no parallel in grandeur
  Has many praiseworthy traits, both inherited
   and acquired.
  He is a branch whose tree stems back to the time
   of Noah, and he is a garden which diffuses
   its refreshing perfume.

Are panegyrics by any panegyrists suitable for anyone
Except the generous lords, the Banū Ṣumādiḥ?
They are luminaries of good omen.
  They are the most noble, great, and proudest princes.
  They possess glory that is pure, so they are especially
   suited to praise.

Although Muḥammad is far away, desire for him is near,
And around him soldiers from his family respond
As if they were lions in the thick of battle.
When they draw their sharp-edged swords, then prepare
for the death of deaths,
And victory, and conquests, and a sign which appears.

When Ibn Ma^{c}n appeared with his clamorous army
And called each competitor by name in the challenge,
Then battle sang out while the sword rejoiced,
"How beautiful is the army with its orderly ranks
When the champions call out, 'Oh, Wāthiq, oh, handsome
one!'"

24
Anonymous

Oh, soul so close to me that it could be my
brother, is this love which you
create in me or madness?

I am lost between those who blame and criticize.
I am alone in a state of madness.
I don't think that my heart can bear
What separation demands of my spirit, although
it is neither adversary nor judge.

Oh, gazelle that ran away,
Your eyes have left me forsaken.
They maintain that I will see you tomorrow,
Whereas I think that death will come before tomorrow.
How far from me today is that which they promise!

Come a bit closer, oh, moon.
Bashfulness is about to erase your light.
Is this flirtation or caution?
Do not fear my trick or ambush, for you are a gazelle
and love is sacred territory.

Oh, Hishām of abundant beauty, what kind of passion is this?
Oh, love which finds fault with all other love,
I have found no remedy since I have been away from him.
The glances—each one is a disease—have taught you
to blow on the knots.

Are there, because of my desire, perfumed traces in every Eastern wind
Which a miracle has wondrously revealed
When I sing about you out of deep emotion?
"Oh, gentle breeze from my homeland, ask the loved ones how they are."

25
By Ibn Zuhr

Oh, cupbearer, a complaint is being made to you.
We called you, but you did not listen.

Many a drinking companion have I adored for his fair complexion
While I drank wine from the palm of his hand.
Whenever he woke up from his drunken states,
He pulled the wine skin to him, reclined, and gave me sixteen draughts.

Why was my eye blinded by the sight?
After looking at you, it did not recognize the moonlight.
If you wish, then listen to my story.
My eyes became blind from so much crying, and my body was shaken by sobbing.[32]

He is a branch of a willow, bending from where he stood tall.
The one who loved him died from too much passion,
Quivering within, his strength weakened.
Whenever he considered separation, he cried, "Woe unto him who cries for that which has not happened!"

I have no patience or strength.
Why did my people blame me and work so hard at it?
They did not know why I complain about the one I love.
A state like mine should be complained about—the sadness of despair and the humiliation of longing.

My heart is feverish and tears flow forth.
He knows the sin yet will not acknowledge it.
Oh, you who disclaim what I describe,
My love for you has grown and increased. Don't say, where love's concerned, "I am a claimant!"

26

By Ibn Baqī

I am not free from the captivity of your
love, even though you seek to release me.

I have assumed an obligation to cultivate your love.[33]
Give me security from your eyes,
For I have endured hardship caused by you for quite some time,
Ever since I affectionately laid my hands on the darkness
of the night in which your face became dawn.[34]

Beauty appeared and offered refuge.
The heart refused and therefore fell to pieces.
I am somewhere between this and that.
Ever since you girded yourself with an embellished sword,
you excelled in beauty and inflicted wounds.

Because of your dual conduct, I found myself amid fierce conflicts.
Arabs who made turbans of their hair
Unsheathed the magic of eyelids like quick-cutting swords.
Steadfastness marched towards them, but it fled
when they shook their bodies like spears.

Many a waist became so thin because of you that it is delightful.
He was fastening the sword around him on a belt
And then complained about the hips' burden, for it was hard to bear.
My love, therefore, became transparent and revealed
itself. If only the one who died of love could
be saved!

I do not complain about anything except continued separation,
Since I protected the heart from the censurer's blame
And sang the words of another for them:
"Teach me how to forget, and if not, then
veil my eyes from winsome youths!"

27

By Ibn Baqī

I complain while you know my condition. Isn't
that the essence of the futility and error?

If there is no way to reach you,
Then patience concerning a beautiful thing is becoming,
For time both separates and unites.

Increase your turning away! There is no escape
from the reunion which the passing nights will
grant.

They said, and they did not speak the truth,
"You've spent your youth clowning."
So I said, "If I were determined to repent
While the cup is in the right hand of my gazelle and
the music of the three-stringed lute was high,
then that would be fine."

No, by the One who causes death and life,
No one delights my eye except Yaḥyā
With his nature and his countenance.
So congratulate him and the high posts attained,
which he gathered through magnificence,
beauty, and majesty.

I had doubts about the noble and lofty
Until I saw you, oh, Ibn ᶜAlī.
And when you alighted in the midst of the assembly,
You were like the rising moon when it is full, like
the sea when the tide is rising, abounding with
gifts.

Stand and listen to the young woman with rounded breasts
Who sings what was required in the way of a complaint,
Tearing her hair and gown:
"Alas! What has happened to me! I dallied with
him, and he ruined my dress and my locks of
hair!"[35]

28

Perhaps by Ibn Baqī or al-Aᶜmā al-Tuṭīlī

I was patient, and patience is characteristic
of the miserable.
And I did not say to the one who kept shunning me,
"My suffering is enough for me."

Can anyone but me boast of humiliation? I fell in love with him
while he was at the gathering.
Scorn for people is a religion with him. Poetry is not able to
describe him completely.
Every day I saw him affecting my situation.
My love for him killed me, yet he revived me
With fine teeth which gave me a drink.

My martyrdom consists of dying for him. When he picks roses, as
many as the hand can hold,
Two roses look for the elevated spot and alight in the meadows of
his cheeks.
The wine of eyelids intoxicates him,
And then he passes by me, sober, like one drunk
Amid a herd of young gazelles.

It is now springtime, oh, Yaḥyā, so let me drink from your raised
right hand
A wine which can make me own the world. Don't you see that the earth
is clothed with embroidered cloth,
And blossoms of silver and gold,
And water which resembles a snake gliding along
In the brook of a garden?

Oh, star that appeared from the Banū Qāsim, welcome to your perpetual
good omen.
As to the favors, I am incapable of giving thanks for them in prose
or poetry.
You have made me forget my people and my homeland.
I found sweetmeats in each heavy rain which poured forth
And quenched my thirst.

Just as the wild white antelope condemned man, condemn her.
Her messenger forbade what he forbade,
And anger about her has fallen upon him, so longing has begun to
sing about her:
"Without fail I will appear where he can
see me.
Perhaps he will greet me.
What has happened to me is enough!"

29
Probably by Ibn Baqī

Oh, woe to the lover who looks at lightning
And has a desire to weep with the doves.

Because of being so far from my friends, I have cried blood.
How many from the herd there were mine! What meetings with rouged
figures
When the army of the night had been routed in the West!
Dawn poured forth in the East. It was day.
From the stars of the horizon flowed the turbid
blood of dawn.

My yearning is more worthy for being hesitant, even though it has increased.
Al-Maᶜẓam planned a journey in the council chamber.
I said, when the camel driver started early in the morning and urged the camels on by singing,
"Hold my heart fast with sympathy when they start.
I think that it will break from throbbing so."

In the land of Granada, there is a full moon that has attained perfection.
Poetry obeys him, and so does prose, when he extemporizes.
One of his qualities is noble pride. What ornaments!
How many men desire to have them and cannot.
These are white markings on the legs of the fleetest and white blazes on the face.[36]

With his five fingers he can water a desert as wide as five days' journey.
The sun is put to shame by the sun of his virtues.
Oh, most beautiful of men in kindness towards one who hopes,
From the joyful countenance of your bright face he knew the good news
That wealth would be poured from your fingertips.

When I was crazy about mentioning his name and he was troubling me,
I wrote what yearning dictated to me,
And I cried out, "Oh, how feverish is my heart from illness!
Fate has decided on separation, oh, ᶜAbd al-Ḥaqq,
So desire does not allow me to live and leaves me nothing."

30
By al-Aᶜmā al-Tuṭīlī

He has misgivings about my approaches and is afraid, which is sweeter than security.
In his face is a *sunna*,[37] through which blame is suffocated and choked.

How fantastic is that which he brings forth for those who love him, and that which he takes away!
He has sweet red lips and fine teeth. Inside his mouth is a doctor of the sick, and he can make one happy.
How lovable he is! How lovable! Oh, his false blaming has lasted a long time.

Don't you see my sadness burning like fire in my heart?
That is enough for me as Paradise. Oh, water! Oh, shade! Oh, splendor!

May God protect you from what I encounter! And he has already done so.
Because of you, I am a distraught wanderer, delighting in my misery, and not just a little.
I love to mention his name, whereas he has not spared me nor acted justly.
Full of vanity, he baffles my thoughts, obstructing them.
He attacked, but there was no protection to ward him off nor any spearhead to seize for defense.

Oh, ornament of the world, from all those who try to charm you or honor you
There comes a suggestion of reverential awe. He is afraid of making you notorious if he were to call you by name.
One of the most remarkable things about love is that someone who cannot see you loves you.
If he is asked about you, he makes an allusion. His state tells—and speaks the truth—
That you are the suspect about whom madness hints or talks.

Don't be deceived about me, for it is a matter of endurance or death.
Trust that I worry if fate forsakes or contradicts.
Oh, how ashamed of myself I am! How long shall I entertain vain hopes without receiving anything?
What can I do about it while beauty has a pledge of love which does not grow old?
If you stated that I'm mad, where could I go or what could I do?

I meet you at a distance and only confide in you out of longing.
By God, I don't know why my condition is so difficult and hard to bear where you're concerned.
I sing and have no excuse except to summon you before a judge in order to get an embrace:
"Oh, Lord, how patient I am! I see my heart's beloved and love him passionately.[38]
If only it were the custom to embrace a friend when one sees him!"

31
Probably by al-Aᶜmā al-Tuṭīlī

Love produces the pleasure of blame for you, and rebuke for this
is sweeter than kisses.
Everything is instrumental in causing love. Love became too strong
for me, and yet its origin was but play.
If only good luck were effective, then beauty
would be charitable.

One could swear an oath by that face. Protect it from blame. Truly
it is a sacred place.
Is it lawful in your eyes to shed my blood? Or are your cheeks
embroidered with blood?
A garden bends upon a branch, a branch of a willow
which is supple.

Oh, bright face with which fate has beguiled me, is it the sun in its
radiance or the moon?
These waists are girded with pupils of the eyes which have gazed so long
that they can no longer sleep.
These eyes don't make an exception for any other man nor
do they turn towards anyone else.

The Hawwarah are princes of nations. I set foot in that highest field.
They are stars of Gemini and Aries, which are incomparable and have
become proverbial.
The Banū Qaḥṭān are as generous as the water of rain
clouds. Speak about Ghassān, and don't make allusions.

Oh, distant one to whom my hope has drawn near, far be it from
you to be aroused by greed.
Your servant by the gate, fearful and impatient, calls out. Perhaps
the invocations will be heard.
"Oh, branch of the beech tree, come give me a hand!
Pomegranates taste good to the one who plucks!"[39]

32

By al-Aʿmā al-Tuṭīlī

You are my choice. May God not bring the
slanderers near!

If anyone wants to speak, I will not listen.
I have submitted to loving you, and I am not a person who is usually
so submissive.
It is enough for me that an intercessor of mine is welcomed with your
consent.
I am drunk and sober, between fear and joy.

Oh, one who blames me at length and obtains no advantage from doing so,
How inferior is fresh wine, by God, compared to these good qualities!
Traps of the mind, may they be ransomed, traps that they are.
Is there any sin in indulging my desire for them?

Love of beautiful things is a divine duty and the rest of courtly life
is a *sunna*.[40]
Beauty is temptation, and his charms suffice for beauty.
And who refuses to indulge in courting? Truly he and I
Should be free from the excuses connected with all this.

Who will do justice to me, desiring to draw near to God? And it should
be amazing enough for him
That my beloved should say, when I have considered his vanity to be
rude,
"There is a close relationship between me and some of my lustrous
companions,
And where lances are concerned, I have a certain
pride and exuberance."

As for me, there is nothing left of my heart
From that long period when I tried to protect it. My eye has been emptied
Out of a desire, from which there is no escape or death,
To reveal its secret, which is forbidden.

Someone else would be shrewd or circuitous when he loved.
Isn't visible sickness and hidden desire enough?
I have been an ascetic, or as I have been, but
Love of beauties corrupted my asceticism
and piety.

33
By Ibn Baqī

Who seeks revenge for the one killed by
gazelles of the litters, the temptresses
of the pilgrims?

They shoot at them with arrows around the sacred house.
The one disfigured by fatigue longs to pluck
perfumed red anemones. She said, "Oh,
you who love me passionately, come!"

She passed by me and I turned pale. She said, "You have loved." I said—
And so the desiring one, departing then from godliness
and the clamor of the pilgrimage, appointed
blazing passion as successor—

"Desire has lasted a long time and my only favor from you was 'No! No!'"
Oh, my friend, tell the camels to turn back. Turn
back, by God, turn back!

You are the king, the chief. You are the precious necklace,
The giver, as noble as fleet horses with fine saddles
in relation to the sons of infidels.

You smile on visitors and strike fiercely with swords,
Oh, *ḥājib*, oh, rainbow-hued plant of basil, and
henna of the meadows.

34
By al-Aʿmā al-Tuṭīlī

He is like a sweet harvest. What harm would
it do him if I were to reap it?
Because of my concern for him, I gather it,
and my distress is my business.

Love of beauty is a religious duty imposed on every free person,
And in flirtation there is an excuse for those who violated chastity.
Is there in union any relief from the long separation,
Or, in being near one another, anything to compensate
for my sorrows,
And in a guarantee that he would stop abusing me?

Is there a way to arrange a meeting by false pretenses?
The sick one is breathing his last and the soul leaves the body
  slowly.[41]
What is the stern censurer compared to my lovesickness and my longing?
    I can only see myself turning my reins
    Away from pretty girls, for I do not have a second heart.

ᶜAlī has been raised to commandership over the Muslims.
He is a clear morning that delights the mind and the eyes.
Generous and proud, he satisfies you in strength and gentleness.
    He is like an Indian sword and like the clouds which
      continuously rain,
    One who fulfills desires and fills the eye of the times.

Stop fighting, for he is enough for you in battle.
He is good luck which has been exalted above all lofty things.
He destroys sword blades and shackles heroes.
    He is like time, which does not hesitate.
    Like the sun, he draws near despite the remoteness of
      the place.

Bring the good news, for this is easy.
This sign satisfied them and satisfied you.
As to the emirate, listen to it when it sings:
    "How he has astounded me, oh, people!
      How he has afflicted me!
    How he has provoked me! I will barter
      my beloved for another."

CHAPTER THREE
Commentary on Ibn Sanā' al-Mulk's Andalusian Anthology

The poems in this Andalusian anthology contain a variety of moods and themes which are typical of classical Arabic poetry, as Ibn Sanā' al-Mulk stated in his theoretical discussion of the *muwashshaḥ*. In this collection, the main thematic distribution consists of the following categories: 80 percent of the poems contain love lyrics, 50 percent have panegyric stanzas, and 20 percent include bacchic verses. Each poem is apt to contain more than one theme, and the poets freely weave diverse *topoi* together to achieve some stunning effects.

Wine, love, and nature themes meld to form some of the most delightful lyrics in the anthology, as can be seen in the third and fourth *muwashshaḥs*. Both poems are highly stylized and have a number of features in common. Their setting couldn't be more charming: a fresh garden or meadow, still moist from the night dew and early morning rains. Bright flowers abound and a stream ripples like a coat of mail. It is a luxuriant cultivated area, probably not unlike the gardens around the Alhambra or those being excavated at Madīna al-Zahra outside of Cordova. The natural environment has been manicured and tamed, but nature still plays an active role. The breeze "has clothed the river with a coat of mail," "weeping clouds have made the flowers laugh," "the hand of the rain untied the buds of the blossoms," and the sun "pulled out lightninglike swords on the horizon." The role that nature plays is limited and personified, sometimes that of a gentle mother, at other times that of a warrior brandishing his sword. There is no sublime awe inspired by these acts, no direct confrontation between the poet and his universe. It is as if the poet's cultural inheritance had put blinders on him, making it impossible to see beyond the scope of previously trodden poetic paths. Yet within the confines of this tradition, each poet has his own personal vision which modifies that which has been written before. This infinite number of variations on a theme is one of the joys of Arabic poetry. The baroque fugue might be considered a musical counterpart. The central bars of each fugue are generally original and the number of variations is usually confined to that one piece, whereas in much Middle Eastern poetry the themes seem to be limited and the variations are infinite. If one accepts the Bergsonian view that no two people see the same object or incident in precisely the same way, due to the differences in both their subjective and objective vantage points, this individuating aspect of Arabic poetry becomes a source of unending interest.

Another variation on this setting is found in poem No. 28:

> It is now springtime, oh, Yaḥyā, so let me drink from
> your raised right hand
> A wine which can make me own the world. Don't you see that
> the earth is clothed with embroidered cloth,
> And blossoms of silver and gold,
> And water which resembles a snake gliding along
> In the brook of a garden?

Here again nature, wearing embroidered robes, is personified, and flowers have been forged of precious metals rather than their own fragile petals. Andalusia must have been very green and flower-laden in the spring, quite unlike the dry desert homes of the Arabs who made their way to Spain. The images which springtime evokes in their poetry and the emphasis on nature's beauty, petrified as it may be, indicates that the climate had an effect on poetic vision there. I encountered a lovely description in a short *muwashshaḥ* by Ibn Zuhr which seems to be derived from such first hand observation and experience:

> Why doesn't the infatuated one recover from his
> drunkenness? Oh, how drunk he is—without wine!
> Why does the sad one, filled with longing, mourn
> for his homeland?

> Do you recall our days by the canal, and our nights?
> Did the musk of our dwelling place benefit from the sweet-
> smelling breeze?
> Or was the beauty of the splendid place about to revive us?

Tall, elegant trees shade the meadow with leafy branches.
Water flows, and swimming, immersed in the water,
are leaves of sweet basil.[1]

The imagery here is sketchy, but the visual picture of a canal running through a meadow whose trees contrast with delicate leaves of basil immersed in flowing water is given an additional dimension through Ibn Zuhr's recollection of fragrances. There was a redolent breeze, the mild minty odor of basil, and heavy musk in the air. These few details enable us to re-create a whole scenario in our minds.

Very often the poet's companions are called to drink at sunrise. In poem No. 4, the sun appears before the people's eyes, and the "hand of the East and the West" in No. 3 refers to the rising and setting sun which is filling the horizon with swords of light at dawn. In *muwashshaḥ* No. 16, the poet calls out:

Come early for wine and smell the flowers!
Life is worthless as long as there is no intoxication.
Seldom do I forgo sipping from the drinking cups
While a bewitching glance is helping at the social gathering.
So give me the daughter of the vine to drink!

This anonymous author is following an established bacchic tradition made famous by such Middle Eastern poets as ᶜUmar Khayyām, Abū Miḥjan, and Abū Nuwās. It was also followed by other Andalusian writers like Ibn Hazm who wrote verses in praise of wine one moment and a few lines later declared that he'd never tried it.[2] Within the confines of this tradition, the verses have been highly stylized and refined for a sophisticated audience. Many wholesome rough grains of daily life have been removed, but not all. The fact that Muslims were not allowed to drink alcohol did not stop them from referring to the Christian monasteries, convents, and taverns where it was made or sold. One poet revealingly alluded to wine as the "daughter of the monastery," an appropriate mutation of the common metaphor, daughter of the vine or jug.

Parallels between alcoholic intoxication and amorous intoxication also form part of the Andalusian poets' repertoire. In the above *muwashshaḥ* by Ibn Zuhr, the lover finds himself in a drunken state that was caused by passion rather than wine. Poets, philosophers, and moralists alike knew that turbulent emotions could upset a person's equilibrium as easily as alcohol and that the effects were often similar.[3] Extremes of joy or sorrow inebriate the psyche, as in poem No. 20, where the lovesick poet is overcome by anguish and confesses:

I have no wine but sorrow.
Mixing with it in the cup are tears
which flow continuously.

This substitution of sorrow for wine and tears for water is a poignant variation of the usual mixing of water and wine, a typical version of which can be seen in the opening lines of Ibn al-Labbāna's *muwashshaḥ*, No. 12.

> Thus the light of the shining stars leads the way
> To the seated ones when water is mixed with wine
> in the glasses.

Here the stars stand for glimmering bubbles which form when the wine and water are mixed together.

Other poets struggle with the temptations of wine but are overcome, celebrating gay occasions or else drowning their sorrows in the glass. The theme of repentance occurs frequently in Arabic verse, but in the Almoravid *muwashshaḥ*, No. 5, it is treated quite lightly, more like an excuse to present the *kharja*. The opening stanzas are blatantly bacchic:

> Pass us the drinking glass to help us forget the
> passion of love,
> And summon the companions, as friendship requires.
>
> Submit to desire like a law as long as you live, oh, my friend.
> Don't listen to the speech of one who blames you,
> For it is a rule that wine should be brought to you by one with
> Fingertips of jujube and candied fruit of the rose,
> Bordered by two locks of myrtle which curve around
> the cheek.

The possibility of abstinence under these circumstances seems most unlikely, as the closing taunt indicates:

> While I was drinking a pure beverage,
> I was repenting, but still wavering,
> When a friend from the group of aesthetes said to me,
> "Our companion has repented. Sing and serenade him!
> Present him with the drinking cup. Perhaps he will
> relapse."

These lines are clear, but I think that the second *qufl* may need some explanation. Since jujube trees do not grow in the American temperate zone, it helps to know that the jujube is a small, reddish datelike fruit, often compared to fingertips of beautiful women. "Candied fruit of the rose" refers to the cheek, a well-established metaphor in Arabic poetry, while "locks of myrtle" stand for locks of hair that curve about the face, not a garland or green adornment on top of the head. In contrast to Western writers, an Arabic poet takes for granted that the people who hear his poetry are already familiar with the stock metaphors. Assuming this, he will sometimes construct quite elaborate imagery based on metaphors already known. In other words, he can deal with truth not only once or twice removed, but three times removed, if one considers this from a platonic point of view.

Later in the same *muwashshaḥ*, it is hard to tell whether or not the poet is praising a ruler whose reign is truly blessed by prosperity and open generosity, or whether he is declaring this with the hope of receiving financial remuneration afterward. Unless born to wealth, the poets depended on such sources for their livelihood. Hyperbole and flattery must have turned the leaders' heads, or else we would not find so much of it in these poems. After the stanzas praising Abū Bakr Yaḥyā, the poet brusquely dismisses the subject and returns to the narrative of his past, injecting a few lines about his attempt to avoid wine in favor of God's rules of temperance. As to his answer to the leader's taunting challenge to forsake his return to religious principles, we are left with no doubt in our minds. The opening lines clearly spell out the philosophy by which he has chosen to guide his life.

In none of these *muwashshaḥs* does wine play a central role. Returning to poems No. 3 and No. 4, we see how the poets have blended the bacchic theme with impressions of nature's morning colors. They then move on to laments of unrequited love. Ḥātim ibn Sa^cīd, author of the third *muwashshaḥ*, abruptly shifts into another mode with the exclamation, "Behold! I have a lord who has dominated, has made himself master." We hesitate a moment, almost hoping that he will continue in the same pleasant mood, but a few lines later we are plunged into a tumultuous flood of tears which cannot drown the burning coals of his passion. The anonymous poet of No. 4 is similarly tearful, but has handled the transition more gently. The rising sun, referred to in the second stanza, is "eclipsed by a veil of darkness." This creates a disconsolate tone for the lines which follow. Here passion itself tyrannizes. His tears are of no avail against the onslaught of his grief caused by a faithless and merciless beloved who has abandoned him. Under these circumstances, he sings out the *kharja* of another person in love: "My darling, you are my neighbor, your house is next to mine, yet you are avoiding me." The transition from the main body of Ḥātim ibn Sa^cīd's poem to the *kharja* is equally smooth, for he explains that he replied to the censurers who blamed the beloved for his behavior: "Perhaps he has an excuse while you are blaming." In both *muwashshaḥs*, the poet himself recites the *kharja*, although in the former instances, he claimed that it was the song of another. In fact, over half of the *kharjas* in this collection issue from the mouth of the poet, a point which will be taken up in Chapter V.

The anthology is not totally devoid of *muwashshaḥs* that fit the formula of a female introducing the *kharja*, which is characteristic of so many *muwashshaḥs* with a Mozarabic ending. Poem No. 27, by Ibn Baqī, a man who also wrote Mozarabic *kharjas*, is a good example:

> Stand and listen to the young woman with rounded breasts
> Who sings what was required in the way of a complaint,
> Tearing her hair and gown:

> "Alas! What has happened to me! I dallied with
> him, and he ruined my dress and my locks of
> hair!"

The young woman's lament in this *kharja* mirrors the poet's lovesick tone at the beginning of the poem. Only Ibn Baqī's faith in the shifting moods of fate, brought about by the eternal flow of time, saves him from total desolation in this poem. Patience is valued, as he firmly believes that circumstances will change eventually and grant him his wish. When censurers criticize his youthful foolishness, he indicates that he has no inclination to repent. The time to renounce worldly pleasures is while the going is good, while the wine is being passed. This, he implies, he could not do. In the panegyric section, the stock images which describe Ibn ᶜAlī's magnificence are handled well and with moderation.

> I had doubts about the noble and lofty
> Until I saw you, oh, Ibn ᶜAlī.
> And when you alighted in the midst of the assembly,
> You were like the rising moon when it is full, like
> the sea when the tide is rising, abounding with
> gifts.

After this passage, Ibn Baqī does not provide a transition leading into the *kharja*; but if the mind retains the earlier stanza depicting a cup in the right hand of a gazelle and the music of the lute, then the continuity of the poem is not likely to be missed. Whether the singer of the *kharja* is the poet himself or a young woman accompanied by the lute, the concerned voice is particularly feminine and disillusioned.

In this poem, time is a consoling factor, for Ibn Baqī has faith in the eternal flux which brings both joy and sorrow. Al-Tuṭīlī's tone in the first *muwashshaḥ* of the anthology is more mournful.

> Woe unto me for what I suffer! My afflictions make me so
> thin that people can see through me.
> He is so inconsistent with me, sometimes violent, other
> times slow and deliberate.
> Whenever I said, "Enough!" he would say to me, "How can
> you be so sure?"

Al-Tuṭīlī has been teased by his beloved's inconsistent behavior. He is about to go mad, "releasing the reins" of his troubled mind. The firm exclamation, "I must have you," followed by the imperative, "Take my heart, humbly given," accents the urgency within. His sudden shift from a rather impersonal description, conventionally but delightfully phrased, to the immediacy of the second person startles appropriately. He reverts back to the third person, continuing his lonely narrative until he reaches the hopeless fatality of the *kharja*, where the beloved sings to him:

> "I have seen that you are sick.
> What's wrong with you? You know
> Time will pass
> And you will forget me."

Al-Tuṭīlī's adherence to standard imagery makes it difficult to know whether or not his emotions are anything more than a poetic attitude adopted by convention, a phenomenon encountered in so much of this poetry. I think it may be futile to ask, for any art which adheres to strict stylistic devices does not encourage individualized expression of emotion or vision. As in the case of medieval Christian painting or sculpture, there were styles that predominated for long periods of time. Each artist or craftsman channeled his unique abilities along these established lines. Therefore, if we could look at the total number of *muwashshaḥs* as we look at a particular workshop or school of Italian painting, I think that the problem of stock imagery and emotional concepts would be better understood.

It is also wise to keep in mind the fact that these poets were paid by the rulers and wealthy patrons to whom their verses were sung. Like commissioned artisans, they were rewarded in accordance with the pleasure they gave to men with fixed ideas of what constituted a good poem or song, rulers who had been educated in a certain way and whose literary horizons probably did not go beyond that tradition. The drawbacks of this system became apparent when the North African commander, Yūsuf ibn Tāshfīn, conquered al-Andalus during the last decade of the eleventh century. He displaced talented poet-kings like al-Muᶜtamid of Seville and al-Muᶜtaṣim of Almería, who had generously supported the region's poets because of their own deep appreciation and fondness for Arabic poetry. In sharp contrast, Ibn Tāshfīn did not understand the intricacies of Arabic literature, since his native language was Berber. As a result, Andalusian court poets suddenly lost their liberal benefactors and found themselves obliged to curry favor among a less educated class of people. The subsequent relaxation of literary standards may be one of the reasons why the *muwashshaḥ* gained prominence during the Almoravid period and was finally included in the anthologies of esteemed authors like Ibn Bassām.[4] Until then, the *muwashshaḥ* had not been accepted by highly educated scholars and had been looked down upon because of its popular nature.

Perhaps in an effort to win approval, occasional attempts were made to imitate archaic, but still highly respected themes from pre-Islamic odes. The first part of *muwashshaḥ* No. 7 exemplifies this type of imitation. It begins with a bereaved poet recalling his past love at the site of an old encampment, where only a few traces remain.

Skeletal traces of the encampment revive
my sorrow. Is it possible
To find solace for my longing heart?
Die, oh, consolation!

Oh, vestige which predestined my death,
You were thirsty. Here are the tears of my eye
Which pour forth, so quench your thirst at the fountain.
But oh, you who have departed, you are to blame
for my sin. Perhaps the time has come
For me to die. Then woe! Alas!

Had this been written by a Bedouin in the desert, it might be convincing, but life in al-Andalus had little in common with the nomadic tribal life of Arabia. Despite the fact that this pre-Islamic theme is found in classical Arabic *qaṣīdas* from al-Andalus, it seems totally out of place here. Such hackneyed lines are, happily, the exception rather than the rule in the Andalusian *muwashshaḥs* that I have read.

Ibn Baqī uses another traditional Islamic motif in poem No. 33.

Who seeks revenge for the one killed by gazelles
of the litters, the temptresses of the
pilgrims?

They shoot at them with arrows around the sacred house.
The one disfigured by fatigue longs to pluck
perfumed red anemones. She said, "Oh,
you who love me passionately, come!"

The gazelles are women taking part in a pilgrimage, travelling in litters for protection. As can be seen in this poem, pilgrimages to the holy cities of Islam provided opportunities for romantic as well as religious experiences.[5] On such occasions, the virtue of continence was apt to be replaced by compliance with the temptress' desire. Good Muslims were, of course, enjoined to turn their eyes away from women who could arouse their lust, but the temptation to look was as difficult to resist.[6] This pilgrim succumbed:

And so the desiring one, departing then from
godliness and the clamor of the pilgrimage,
appointed blazing passion as successor.

An unusual extended metaphor occurs in *muwashshaḥ* No. 14. After several stanzas of pleasant description at the beginning, there is a long passage equating the poet's state with that of a hunted hare. This has been extremely well executed. In the second *bait*, for instance, the hunter's easy sway and leaning towards generosity give not only an impression of his character but also of his slender, willowy build, an allusion to the stock metaphor of a person's torso seeming like a supple bough. The last line of that stanza refers to a miraculous metamorphosis. Descriptions of a gazelle hunting lions are frequently encountered, as in poem No. 12: "He is a gazelle who hunted the strongest lions with harsh glances which penetrate the homes of people." Here, more spectacularly, a true transformation takes place and suddenly a devouring beast appears where a soft fawn had been. This fits in well with the strong nature of the man being eulogized, whose prowess as a hunter is indicated. The following scene of the hunt is terribly immediate. The hunter has forsaken the poet, and even to hope for a change of heart strikes him as futile. The blow is therefore final, like being cut through the jugular vein by the grasping teeth of hounds. The blood dripping from the wounded hare is his reservoir of life, which will soon be spent. Sparrow hawks dive to devour the helpless remains. When the gruesome beauty of the ritual ends, the poet returns to his description of Ibn Ṣaddīn Abū al-Walīd. Yet this great man does not conduct himself honorably. "In regard to the hunt, he acts according to the old tricks." He kills and then goes away. The imagery of the *kharja* provides a superb ending to this haunting poem.

> The gazelle crosses the plain and the greyhounds
> hasten behind.
> My sadness is nothing but guilty intentions which
> almost succeeded, but they did not overtake him.

There are a number of *muwashshaḥs* devoted to the praise of rulers, whose *kharjas* seem to have been written by the poet with specific men in mind. The language is far from colloquial, and names are woven into the final verses. No. 21, by Ibn ᶜUbāda, is a good example of this. The opening *matla*ᶜ plays with the metaphor of a smile, which is as bright as a bolt of lightning and whose teeth are pearls or hailstones symmetrically arranged. The opposition between passionate fire and tears is commonly found in this love poetry, although it is treated somewhat differently in each new context, as the translations reveal. Certain linguistic overtones can never be rendered by translations, however. The following line from Ibn ᶜUbāda's poem illustrates this point quite clearly: "So my sorrows catch fire and burn fiercely." A second definition from the Arabic root for sorrows (*sh-j-n*) is "twigs" or "branches." Both meanings probably would be known to the Arabic-speaking listener, and the image of burning twigs would remain in the background to heighten the impact of the phrase. Another noteworthy feature of this *muwashshaḥ* is the celebration of two rulers who have recently been reconciled, al-Muᶜtaṣim of Almería and al-Muᶜtadid of Seville. The impression of a strong bond between them is reinforced by the images of rope being tied, a solid structure which will not crumble, and eternal columns which cannot fall. If the political reality had been as firm as Ibn ^{c}Ubāda would like us to believe, Muslim Spain would not have fallen apart so rapidly under the pressure of internal struggles and the threat of advancing Christianity from without. The poet trades on the emirs' taste for hyperbole, I assume, and comes up with some resounding lines of praise. The *kharja*, presented in the form of a rhetorical question, is introduced by doves who inhabit the forests of these politically reunited lands. Their song implies that past generations never experienced or even expected two rulers as grand as these.

Another *muwashshaḥ* written by Ibn ^{c}Ubāda is devoted to al-Mu^{c}taṣim alone. After a few amorous opening stanzas, he uses an unusual transitional enjambment, which runs not just between lines but between *bait* and *qufl*. He quickly moves from the theme of love to praise.

So I said, questioning, "Who made
My heart throb?" So he said, "Stand and perceive on the shore
The banners of the ships of war and seek information from the pendants."

Almería at that time was a thriving seaport and the capital of al-Mu^{c}taṣim's emirate, which makes the imagery of ships, banners, and shoreline extremely appropriate and realistic. A visionary sketch is then presented, depicting masts that are higher than the stars, along with a great man whose ambitions are far above the Pleiades and whose stature reaches beyond Saturn or Jupiter. Stars of good fortune protect him and his kingdom which extends as far as the Christians' towers. His display of naval force, of shining lances on a burning sea, overwhelms the onlooker, yet al-Mu^{c}taṣim's subjects live as if under the spell of a perpetual holiday. We are being inundated by hyperbole again, but this time it seems credible. Perhaps this is due to the fact that Ibn ^{c}Ubāda chose a servant to exclaim the *kharja*, leaving us with the impression that this might be exactly the way a wide-eyed servant would interpret what he saw, even though his choice of words in real life would be less artistic.

The eleventh *muwashshaḥ*, which was probably composed by Ibn al-Labbāna, is dedicated to the ^{c}Abbādid family which governed Seville from 1023 to 1091. When considering this eminent family, the poet inquires:

Who will enable me to do justice in praising the Banū ^{c}Abbād and thanking them adequately?
Those gifts which they gave me were very unexpected. I forgive the one who envies me because of them.

The fact that this dynasty appreciated poets and was generous when it came to remunerating them becomes apparent when the author states that the Banū ^{c}Abbād had provided his wings with feathers. This vivid metaphor indicates that they had made him a wealthy man. A secure life under ^{c}Abbādid rule allowed poets like Ibn al-Labbāna time for lyrical composition. Although they continued their craft despite the political upheaval after al-Muᶜtamid's capture and imprisonment in North Africa, the climate became much more difficult for such artists. This *muwashshaḥ* was undoubtedly written before the Almoravid invasion, for the poet speaks about a time of prosperity in which life is so pleasant that "words of love and youth" are inevitably brought to mind. In this capricious way, he leads us directly into the *kharja*:

> "Send the greeting with the wind for an anxious
> lover who does not trust mankind."

Talking to the wind as if it were a messenger is a common theme in Arabic poetry, and it provides an additional example of the personification of nature discussed earlier. The delightful *kharja* could easily have been taken from another source, but it is probably the poet's original adaptation of the theme. Another version of this is found at the end of No. 24, where an anonymous poet asks:

> Are there, because of my desire, perfumed traces in
> every Eastern wind
> Which a miracle has wondrously revealed
> When I sing about you out of deep emotion?
> "Oh, gentle breeze from my homeland, ask the
> loved ones how they are."

In this particular poem, the poet laments his absent beloved and does not complicate the picture by eulogizing his patron. Because of this, the *kharja* harmonizes well with the whole *muwashshaḥ*, whose tone is more consistent than most.

In the twelfth *muwashshaḥ*, Ibn al-Labbāna again praises the Banū ᶜAbbād and specifically singles out the son of al-Muᶜtamid, ᶜUbaid Allāh Rashīd. Beginning with a few bacchic verses celebrating the reunion of friends who have gathered together to enjoy themselves, he moves on to a charmingly stylized description of the wine bearer, portrayed as a young gazelle. He then proceeds to discuss the sea, which is a standard metaphor for a great man. According to him, ᶜUbaid Allāh Rashīd's fame and qualities surpass those of famed ᶜAbbāsid ruler of Baghdad, Hārūn al-Rashīd. Needless to say, the Andalusian prince has not weathered the test of history like Hārūn al-Rashīd, but such flattery must have delighted the ᶜAbbādid court at the time. Other extravagant claims are made concerning ᶜUbaid Allāh's glory before the poet returns to the theme of the whole family's generosity, which he lauds in the final stanza.

Nobility is yours and you are from a noble family.
All see the attainment of favours they hope for through you,
So the one who sings does not leave in his former condition.
"Banū ᶜAbbād, because of you we are enjoying festivals
And weddings. May you live forever for the people's
sake!"

The *kharja* conveys the impression of universal gratitude and goodwill towards the ruling family. This, too, must have been written before the dynasty's downfall in 1091.

It is clear that Ibn al-Labbāna expected to be handsomely rewarded for his poems; but from the sampling we have of his work in this anthology, it seems that he was more subtle about it than other authors, one of whom wrote *muwashshaḥ* No. 17. The poet may have been Ibn Baqī, but no one is sure. It is certain, however, that he composed a well balanced poem that moves easily from its opening lyrical stanzas to a clever bid for remuneration. To understand the first line, one needs to be aware of the fact that the specific type of visitors mentioned come to see sick people. They often appear in such contexts as this. Later on the poet indicates that he is ill, thereby justifying the first verse, and implies that only his beloved can cure him. Just a glance would suffice, he affirms, although he would really like to receive some wholehearted warmth and generous concern. Here the poet uses generosity as a bridge between the two parts of the *muwashshaḥ*, passing on to praise Abū ᶜAbbās Aḥmad, one of the Banū Qāsim. By flattering Aḥmad's proud spirit of openhandedness, the poet spurs his competitive streak. He even uses legal terms to convey the expectation that he will get what he wants in the line where he states, "My hope judges that he will rule in my favor." The *kharja* is an exclamation confirming Ahmad's magnificence and challenging the Eastern Arabic world to find another man who measures up to him.

"Don't you see that Aḥmad cannot be surpassed
in his great glory?
The West gave rise to him. So show us the likes
of him, oh, East!"

This also reflects the Andalusian's pride in his region. It is an effective *muwashshaḥ* and apparently was well known in its own time. Although there is always more that could be said, it seems appropriate now to look at this collection from another point of view and compare its Arabic *muwashshaḥs* with the ones which contain bilingual *kharjas*.

PART TWO

Comparative Study of Arabic and Bilingual *Muwashshaḥs*

CHAPTER FOUR
Basic Similarities

Before 1948, little attention had been focused on Andalusian *muwashshaḥs*. At that time, however, a startling discovery by Samuel M. Stern revealed the existence of bilingual *muwashshaḥs* with *kharjas* that had been composed in the archaic Romance dialect of al-Andalus, known as Mozarabic.[1] Poets and scholars alike were delighted. They have been busy interpreting these beautiful but puzzling verses ever since, for these recently discovered *kharjas* are important precursors of later Romance lyrics which follow similar traditional patterns.[2] Then in 1965, Emilio García Gómez published a collection of Arabic *muwashshaḥs* with Mozarabic *kharjas* which he had culled from the works of two fourteenth-century Andalusian writers, Ibn al-Khaṭīb and Ibn Bushrā.[3] For the first time, we were able to appreciate each Mozarabic *kharja* as an integral part of a whole poem. The publication of these bilingual texts was a valuable contribution, and I have used García Gómez's edition as a basis for comparison with the Arabic anthology compiled by Ibn Sanā' al-Mulk.[4]

If one were to read only the first four strophes of the Arabic and bilingual *muwashshaḥs*, it would probably be impossible to tell the two collections apart. Perhaps this is partly due to the fact that four of the six known authors in Ibn Sanā' al-Mulk's anthology are represented in the anthologies of Ibn Bushrā and Ibn al-Khaṭīb also. Al-Aᶜmā al-Tuṭīlī, the blind bard of Tudela (d. 1126), and the eleventh-century poet, Ibn ᶜUbāda, are featured in Ibn Bushrā's manuscript. Ibn al-Labbāna (d. 1113) is represented in *Jaish al-Tawshīḥ* by Ibn al-Khaṭīb. Poems by Ibn Baqī (d. ca. 1150) are also found in both. These men have been identified with certainty as the authors of thirteen *muwashshaḥs* in Ibn Sanā' al-Mulk's collection, and twelve additional *muwashshaḥs* have been attributed to them. This makes a total of twenty-five, or about two-thirds of the Arabic corpus selected by Ibn Sanā' al-Mulk. The same poets wrote a total of twelve bilingual *muwashshaḥs*, to which one more, possibly written by Ibn ᶜUbāda, might be added. These comprise approximately one-third of the bilingual corpus taken from Ibn Bushrā and Ibn al-Khaṭīb. Even without this overlapping authorship, there would be little reason to suspect vast differences between the two groups because the main parts of the *muwashahaḥs* are written in classical Arabic and feature such traditional themes as love, wine, and panegyrics. On the whole, basic similarities are easy to find.

The theme of love predominates in these *muwashshaḥs*, and the imagery used to depict the state of the lover and his beloved seems to stem from a common heritage, Arabic love poetry (*ghazal*). Within the body of Arabic literature, the amatory preludes (*nasīb*) of the pre-Islamic odes (*qaṣīda*) contain the oldest lyrical love poetry. *Ghazal*, however, developed during the early Islamic and ᶜUmayyad period and continued into the ᶜAbbāsid age. By the time *muwashshaḥs* were created, love poetry had become a separate genre, the subject of shorter poems which existed independently from the long classical odes.[5] Poets in al-Andalus were undoubtedly influenced by this rich tradition. This, along with the fact that the Andalusian poets share similar political and cultural backgrounds, may help to explain why certain images and points of view are found scattered throughout various collections of *muwashshaḥs*.

In most cases, the poet portrays himself as a scorned but worthy lover, suffering from a terminal case of lovesickness. The symptoms may be any of the following: insomnia, emaciation, madness, humiliation, loss of patience, despair, rivers of tears which can't extinguish flames of passion, a willingness to offer one's own father as ransom for the beloved, or even abjuring Islam to worship a willowy sweetheart. This excessive passion (*hawā*) was considered blameworthy by ethically minded Muslims of the period, and whole treatises were devoted to the problem.[6] One looks in vain for such philosophizing in secular *muwashshaḥs*. The victims of these overwhelming emotions are apt to complain bitterly about their situation, as in poem No. 6 from Ibn Sanā' al-Mulk's anthology.

> What's the use of yearning, which makes the eye shed tears
> and fills the heart with ardor?
> How can you see my illness and still pretend ignorance of
> my love?

Similarly, in No. X[7] from Ibn Bushrā's manuscript, another poet states:

> Whenever I complain to you about my suffering,
> You reply with nothing but laughter.

These wronged lovers often claim that they have been driven insane, as in the last line quoted above, or in No. XXXVII, where Ibn Labbūn states that his beloved has beguiled his reason and destroyed all feeling. Both the poet's reason and religion have been plundered in No. XVIII. Returning to Ibn

Sanā' al-Mulk's Arabic *muwashshaḥs*, the anonymous poet of No. 22 queries, "Who could mean as much to me as this slender one who disturbs the mind?" Still another unknown author describes a similar plight in No. 24:

I am lost between those who blame and criticize.
I am alone in a state of madness.
I don't think that my heart can bear
What separation demands of my spirit, although
it is neither adversary nor judge.

Oh, gazelle that ran away,
Your eyes have left me forsaken.
They maintain that I will see you tomorrow,
Whereas I think that death will come before tomorrow.
How far from me today is that which they promise!

Whenever patience is at its ebb, a discreet and noble lover tries to maintain a stoic stance and proclaims that he will not give up. Al-Tuṭīlī's expression of this attitude in *muwashshaḥ* No. 1 is typical: "I have no patience left but nonetheless will keep on striving." Within the circumscribed range of these carefully delineated emotions, patience is considered to be one of the conditions of suffering. Poets are entitled to boast heroically about their endurance, as in No. 28. Al-Kumait al-Gharbī, in No. XIII, affirms that if his affair is lofty, then his patience has been all the more sublime. Those who fall prey to despair because they can't bear the strain any longer, which is the case in Nos. IV and VIIb, or because there is no hope of receiving any affection from the beloved, as in No. IX, deserve pity and consolation.

The eloquent silence described in *muwashshaḥ* No. 6 is another worthy virtue which forms part of this courtly spirit in Arabic literature. By remaining silent, a man gives evidence of inner strength. At the same time, silence also serves a social function. In order to avoid exposure to demeaning gossip, it was considered more discreet to conceal the beloved's name. Concerning this tradition, Ibn Ḥazm explains, "Sometimes the reason for concealment is that the lover wishes to spare his beloved; then it is a proof of loyalty, a mark of true nobility of character."[8] Illicit love, to which many poets alluded, was not looked upon favorably. Men might even be banished for making such allusions.[9] So one's passions should be kept secret forever, as al-Tuṭīlī advocates in *muwashshaḥ* No. II from Ibn Bushrā's manuscript.

All too often the poet is forced to reveal his love. Ibn Ḥazm comments that "disclosure is sometimes due to love's overpowering mastery; publicity prevails over modesty. In such a case, a man is quite unable to control himself or regulate his actions. This is one of the furthest extremes which passionate love can reach."[10] The anonymous poet of No. IV explains that he had tried very hard to keep the secret, but when he had been given wine to relieve the exhausting tension, he confessed, stating, "Truly, pure wine discloses all bosom secrets." In No. XXXIV, al-Manīshī wonders how long he can go on concealing the pain which has been consuming him for so long that he looks like a ghost.

> If only I could hide it!
> Then my condition would not become known.
> If only my grief would not become evident
> And reveal my innermost thoughts!

Trying to suppress one's complaints often makes matters worse. It can make the anguish more acute and cause everything to become more obvious in the end. Tears well forth and display the grief that had been harbored within. Hātim ibn Saᶜīd laments in poem No. 3 that if it had not been for his tears, which uncovered the secret, his conduct would have been perfectly discreet. Nevertheless, crying may provide some relief, as al-Saraqusṭī describes in the third *qufl* of No. XXVIIIb, found in *Jaish al-Tawshīḥ*.

> There is no help
> Except for tears
> Which come to my eye
> Nor aid
> Except for wailing.

Consequently we find tears flowing like rivers, falling like rain, or glistening like lightning in many *muwashshaḥs*. When these torrents are combined with their opposite, the fire of passion, it is a sign of great emotional turmoil, according to Ibn ᶜUbāda in poem No. 21.

> On the day of parting, in the place of separation,
> Desire offered me two opposites—
> Fire of passion and tears of the eye.
> So my sorrows catch fire and burn fiercely,
> While my eyes overflow continuously with tears.

The degree of intensity implied by such opposition is explained by al-Tuṭīlī in the opening *matlaᶜ* of No. VIII.

> Tears pour forth while ribs are burning. Water
> and fire
> Are not joined together unless the matter is very
> grave.

An idiomatic phrase that expresses a willingness to give one's father as ransom is another indication of strong attachment to the beloved. In No. 13, written perhaps by Ibn al-Labbāna, this idea occurs twice. In the second stanza, he exclaims, "Oh, I'd give my father as ransom for a black-eyed one who is like the full moon." This is soon followed by the verse, "I ransom him, even though it makes me an orphan." In No. XXXI from *Jaish al-Tawishiḥ*, Ibn Arfa[c] Ra'suh expresses this similarly: "I ransom by my father the one whom I love even though he is unaware." The phrase, by my father (*bi abī*), appears frequently in these *muwashshaḥs*; and despite the fact that the verb, to ransom or redeem, is not always given, as in the above *muwashshaḥ*, the prepositional phrase alone generally implies the idea of ransom.

In more extreme cases, the poet may claim that love has totally destroyed his religious belief or that he has oriented his spiritual life around his beloved rather than the sacred Kaaba in Mecca. Ibn Baqī exemplifies this desertion of religious ideals in *muwashshaḥ* No. 33 when he describes a pilgrim who was led astray "from godliness and the clamor of the pilgrimage" by his passionate nature. The anonymous author of No. X calls his beloved a Kaaba of beauty towards which he is making his pilgrimage. Other poets compare their loved ones to the joys of paradise, an image used by al-Manīshī in his bilingual *muwashshaḥ*, No. XXXIV from *Jaish al-Tawshiḥ*, and by the author of No. 7 from Ibn Sanā' al-Mulk's Arabic collection. The *imām*, or religious leader, may also be a simile for the beloved, as in No. XXIII, where she lights the way like an *imām*. Religious images like these are common, despite the fact that their use in this fashion does not conform to the tenets of Islam. They reflect a neoplatonic, mystical mode of thought which was current at the time.[11]

Although certain images might be at variance with orthodoxy, the realities of love were treated with compassion by poets and philosophers alike. It was understood that unwary lovers could suddenly be overcome by a consuming passion, as indicated in the opening stanza of No. 31:

> Love produces the pleasure of blame for you, and rebuke for
> this sweeter than kisses.
> Everything is instrumental in causing love. Love became too
> strong for me, and yet its origin was but play.

The author of these lines is believed to be the blind bard of Tudela, al-Tuṭīlī, who comments about love and religion in two other poems in *Dār al-Ṭirāz*.

> Love of beauty is a religious duty imposed on every
> free person.
> And in flirtation there is an excuse for those who
> violated chastity.

These verses are from *muwashshaḥ* No. 34. A broader statement appears in No. 32, where the following line is found:

> Love of beautiful things is a divine duty and the rest
> of courtly life is a *sunna*.

Here al-Tuṭīlī equates the customs of courtly life with the revered traditions (*sunna*) of the Prophet that every good Muslim is urged to follow. This attitude is entirely in keeping with the mores of a fashionable Islamic elite (*ẓurafā'*) which took great pride in its elegant and refined way of life.[12] Although theologically unsound, these sophisticated values were acceptable within the context of a thriving courtly tradition.[13] Wine was also forbidden by Islamic law, but that prohibition was often ignored by the same people.

Fatalism may have played a part, too, in their willingness to condone moral weakness, as we see in various *muwashshaḥs*. In No. XXV, al-Tuṭīlī again comments, "I was created for love." Ibn Arfaᶜ Ra'suh declares in No. XXXa that fate has caused his beloved to be the victor, so nothing can save him now from the downfall of love. They imply that it is beyond man's power to resist what God has decreed. Because God's will works in mysterious ways, such love may indeed be enlightening and virtuous in the deepest sense of the word, good for the whole being. It would therefore be presumptuous for man to draw a dividing line between earthly and heavenly love.

Apparently, one might just as well be resigned to fate and try to enjoy the situation. A description of such acceptance is expressed by a court poet of Seville at the beginning of *muwashshaḥ* No. 8: "One who is madly in love spends the evening looking at the stars. He finds the pain sweet and is delighted with his states of grief and anxiety." The unknown composer of No. XVI similarly declares, "I am pleased with my humiliation, my illness, and my weariness, so stop criticizing me!" Those who are normally proud and noble find themselves submissive and humbled, a good example of which is found in No. XXXVII, recorded by Ibn al-Khaṭīb. Here the eleventh-century magnate, Abū ᶜĪsā ibn Labbūn, humbles himself before a servant with whom he has fallen in love. He explains that, although he is her lord, love has turned him into her slave. God has willed it, he continues, so there can be no remedy.

Insomnia is one of the worst ailments which is inevitably inflicted upon anxious suitors, and it is frequently accompanied by emaciation. Al-Tuṭīlī complains, "My afflictions make me so thin that people can see through me," in a typical hyperbole from *muwashshaḥ* No. 1. The author of No. 20, possibly Ibn Baqī, describes his predicament in the following manner:

> I said, when he had driven sleep away from me
> And deprived the visitors of all hope because of my disease,
> "Go away from me!" And when he went, I gnashed my teeth.
> My body is so emaciated that one can hardly see it.
> Companions look for it where the moan is.

In *muwashshaḥ* No. XXVIIIa, Ibn Baqī comments more philosophically:

> There is no harm
> In a love which adorns itself
> With garments of emaciation.

It is suitable
For noblemen
And not at all offensive.

Some, who cannot tolerate the strain, turn to wine. "Pass us the drinking glass to help us forget the passion of love." This request forms the opening line of *muwashshaḥ* No. 5; and in No. XXVII, Ibn Baqī states that he must have wine to alleviate the intensity of his torment. This is a more unusual solution to the problem, however. Most suitors seem to prefer pining away to escape through the use of alcohol.

Even death may be looked upon as a relief after this. In fact, it is not unusual to confront death as an ultimate consequence of suffering in the *muwashshaḥs*. This harsh finality conforms to the tradition of ᶜUdhrī poets, men of the ᶜUdhra tribe in Arabia who were famous for loving so passionately that they often died from lovesickness. From a physiological perspective, Ibn Ḥazm has observed that "sometimes the affair becomes so aggravated, the lover's nature is so sensitive, and his anxiety so extreme, that the combined circumstances result in his demise and departure out of this transient world."[14] In the *muwashshaḥs*, this seems more like poetic convention than fact, but even so it is an important motif. *Muwashshaḥ* No. XV opens with the poet dying from grief.

The eyes of a young woman have enslaved my heart.
Who can protect me from the pain of love?
My passion can only end in death.
It's as if my heart were the wing of a sparrow,
Fatally wounded
By arrows aimed at the frightened one
Inexorably.

Imagery involving birds is quite common in these poems, and here the image of a small sparrow arouses feelings of tenderness. A similar plight afflicted al-Khabbāz al-Mursī, author of No. XXXVI.

This turbulent passion is a grave burden for the heart
And has decreed its destruction.
Insomnia has driven away sleep
And it is too late to escape.

In *muwashshaḥ* No. 25 from Ibn Sanā' al-Mulk's collection, Ibn Zuhr describes the state of a man who claims he is dying from an excess of passion. The overall impression is less of a man near death than one afflicted by love-sickness, and many standard symptoms of the disease are manifest.

Why was my eye blinded by the sight?
After looking at you, it did not recognize the moonlight.
If you wish, then listen to my story.
My eyes became blind from so much crying, and my body was shaken by sobbing.

He is a branch of a willow, bending from where he stood tall.
The one who loved him died from too much passion,
Quivering within, his strength weakened.
Whenever he considered separation, he cried, "Woe unto him who cries for that which has not happened!"

I have no patience or strength.
Why did my people blame me and work so hard at it?
They did not know why I complain about the one I love.
A state like mine should be complained about—the sadness of despair and the humiliation of longing.

Although it is confusing to follow the way Ibn Zuhr shifts from the first to the third person in reference to himself, while also using both the second- and third-person singular in connection with his beloved, such changes are typical of this poetry. In the first stanza quoted here, for example, Ibn Zuhr addresses the beloved in the second person and creates an atmosphere of informal dialogue. In the next one, he becomes a narrator telling his own story in the third person. The willow branch is obviously a metaphor for the beloved, who has a lithe, slender figure. In the following series of impersonal pronouns, the poet is referring to himself again as he begins to describe his woeful condition. He has lost all patience and strength to endure. According to al-Tuṭīlī in *muwashshaḥ* No. 30, such an affair reduces itself to a matter of endurance or death. When a man had become so weak and ill that he could resist no longer, death was declared inevitable.

The cause of all this misery is, of course, the beloved, who is normally cruel and unresponsive or else has been separated from the poet. Distance may be a factor in the separation, or the beloved may be too well cloistered. In the former situation, unjust tactics of deception and delay are apt to be used, whereas in the latter, fate may have caused the couple to be apart for long periods or the girl may be closely guarded in the secluded women's quarters of another house. The rhetoric may be simple and direct with a poet openly bewailing his beloved's cruelty, pointing to the harsh effects it has produced and asking for compassion. Complexity may likewise play a part. For instance, one of the most common plays on words concerns the loved one's unjust judgment. In such cases, the poet portrays a judge who is incapable of acting impartially towards the lover. This administrative imagery is a result of the influence of Muslim institutions on the poetry of the period, something which did not exist in pre-Islamic times.[15]

It is sometimes impossible to tell whether the loved ones are male or female, for the stock images used in descriptions hardly change. This is complicated by the fact that masculine pronouns and verb forms are traditionally used in Arabic poetry even when referring to a female figure. Only one woman in the three collections is mentioned by name. She is Hind, addressed by the unknown poet of No. XVIII, from Ibn Bushrā's manuscript. On the other hand, love lyrics are addressed to six males in Ibn Sanā' al-Mulk's anthology, and to another six in the bilingual group, all of whose names are given. This total of twelve does not take into account proper names found in the *kharjas* alone or names of men to whom verses of praise are dedicated, factors which would add another thirty names at least to the list. There are no women of political importance eulogized in any of these *muwashshaḥs*, nor are any female names ever mentioned in the *kharjas*. Nevertheless, it is possible to deduce from comments about the sanctity of the harem or about the beloved's guardian (*raqīb*) that a female is intended. Despite the fact that homosexual love was practiced, it is in keeping with established poetic tradition to assume that the person in question is a young woman when there is no proper noun or other indication to the contrary.

Where descriptions of the beloved are concerned, there is a close similarity between the bilingual and Arabic *muwashshaḥs*. One of the most elegant descriptions is contained in *muwashshaḥ* No. 9 by Ibn ᶜUbāda. This poem, by one of the greatest artists of the genre, presents an excellent picture of the elements which were singled out as desirable features by the people of this culture. The radiance of the sun or moon emanating from the beloved's face is one of the most prevalent images, along with the grace and enchantment of the gazelle. Ibn ᶜUbāda presents the loved one as the ideal archetype after whom the gazelle's lustrous eyes and long neck were patterned. His beauty has reached its apex and, in Aristotelian fashion, need not strive for fulfillment any longer. Pearls, gleaming and white, stand for symmetry and are generally used as a metaphor for perfectly formed and polished teeth. The beloved's face is usually composed of white skin, indicated in this case by jasmine and lilies, and red cheeks, most often depicted as a rose. The mouth may be a little perfume box or a piece of sweet fruit. Eyes flash like swords of an army ready for battle, and the piercing glances are often referred to as arrows, spears, or lances, conquering via sheer sorcery. In this poem Ibn ᶜUbāda compares the beloved's charisma to the highly revered miracle of the Koran, magic considered legitimate only under special circumstances. The torso is slender and willowy and, in general, if a female figure is being represented, the hips tend to be plump and rounded. The image of trailing the train of a robe while walking refers to a dignified, proud bearing. Allusions to the written page are not uncommon and may appear in connection with the smooth surface of the face, as we see here, or in reference to eyebrows that curve like the arched letter *nūn*.

Another strophe describing an unidentified person is in No. XXIIb by Ibn Ruḥaym of Seville, who lived during the twelfth century. This gazelle is definitely a female, whereas the beloved in Ibn ᶜUbāda's *muwashshaḥ* could be either masculine or feminine.

> I ransom by my father the one with perfumed sleeves
> And bewitching glances,
> Rounded breasts and a willowy waist over corpulent hips,
> Who brings together everything that is beautiful
> In a way which cannot be described,
> A full moon surrounded by a night
> Of luxuriant black hair
>
> Under which is a cheek of lilies
> Splashed with musk,
> Embellished with beautiful adornments,
> A joyful countenance, and ornaments.

In *muwashshaḥ* No. XVIII, the only one with a woman's name mentioned, the anonymous poet describes Hind as a gazelle whose beautiful eyes send forth glances like arrows which wound him fatally. He begs someone to bring her to him, for she is the only one who can cure his critical condition. Again and again this motif of the beloved reviving or curing the failing lover surfaces in the *muwashshaḥs*. Since she has caused his suffering, she is the only one who can alleviate it. The standard prescription of a kiss or just a glance is generally enough to satisfy him. As to Hind's physical attributes, she is a branch of a willow that puts all others to shame, one who proudly looks down on the earth beneath her. Teeth like pearls are concealed inside her mouth, and her eyebrows form two graceful *nūns* that curve on her forehead. There is nothing in this short description which we have not seen before.

Two anonymous *muwashshaḥs* are dedicated to young men named Aḥmad. One poem comes from Ibn Sanā' al-Mulk's Arabic anthology; and the other, containing Romance words in its *kharja*, was collected by Ibn Bushrā. An excerpt from the former, No. 13, is given below.

> Oh, I'd give my father as ransom for a black-eyed one
> who is like the full moon.
> He reveals a gem whose kiss is delightful.
> His flowerlike cheek blushes at just a thought,
> So how can I be absolved?
>
> A speckled serpent crept over the brazilwood,
> So don't kiss it!
> By magic he appointed an army of Ethiopians,
> together with Nabateans, to kill heroes.

The time has come to emanate light, like the lord of the mountain,
Like a full moon in darkness, with a body as slim as a reed,
Like a branch of beryl in a rounded hillock of camphor.

The battle mentioned between the Nabateans and the Ethiopians refers to the swordlike glances of Aḥmad's dark eyes attacking the poet and wounding him fatally. This image was drawn from history. The next two have a religious source. The lord of the mountain is Moses, and Aḥmad's beauty has been given to him like a pious endowment (*waqf*). Reeds and branches are typical metaphors for a slender figure. The hillock of camphor combines the visual impression of a rounded shape with the awareness of a pleasant fragrance. Camphor is also a conventional metaphor for white, with black musk as its antithesis. Through this one image, the poet has stimulated one's sense of color, form, and smell. The rest of the poem speaks for itself, reverberating various themes already discussed. The man called Aḥmad in the bilingual poem, No. XIV, must be a blond, because the poet affirms that only blonds can delight him. He then represents the young man metaphorically as a silver branch bursting with leaves of gold, which is a delightful variation of the standard motif. Depicting the hues of his cheek, the poet has created another charming combination.

Bursting forth among anemones is the jasmine of his
cheek,
Streaked with saffron perfume and compound oils of
musk.
And what if I add carnelian to that?

Red anemones have been splashed among white jasmine blossoms instead of roses amid lilies, which are far more frequently seen in these *muwashshaḥs*.

In the fourth strophe of the same bilingual *muwashshaḥ*, the spy (*raqīb*) appears.

While my beloved was sitting by my side,
I complained about my agitation and divulged my grief
So that my physician might see what possessed my heart.
He realized that the spy had approached while
we were unaware,
creeping towards us, and shyness overcame him.

The spy is one stock character who is found only in the bilingual poems, but this must be a matter of sampling because the *raqīb* is a traditional figure mentioned in other Arabic texts.[16] In fact, Ibn Ḥazm devotes a whole chapter in *The Ring of the Dove* to the *raqīb*, which is a good indication of his sociological importance in al-Andalus during the tenth and eleventh centuries at least. There are various kinds of spies described by Ibn Hazm, some who innocently happen to be in the same place that a pair of lovers has chosen in order to be alone, pests who want to find out everything they can about the couple, and those whose duty it is to watch over the beloved. Poets most often refer to the latter type, who can sometimes be won over by conciliation and may then aid the lovers and protect them from danger. But, according to Ibn Ḥazm, "the most disgusting kind of spy is the man who has been tried in love long ago, and suffered its misfortunes over many years . . . he is therefore desirous in the extreme to protect the person over whom he is watching from the calamities of love. God be praised, what a splendid spy he makes, and what mischief stands poised to fall upon lovers through his instrumentality!"[17] Such spies are mentioned often by the authors of the bilingual *muwashshaḥs*. They are generally feared, although the lover may be lucky enough to sneak by in a moment when the *raqīb* is not paying strict attention, as in *muwashshaḥs* No. XI and No. XV. On the whole, he sounds formidable, jealously guarding the beloved from peril, and thereby fanning the flames of romance and intensifying the emotions. He represents a challenge to be overcome rather than an insurmountable barrier which would curtail any further development of a relationship.

The censurer, or reproacher, serves a similar purpose. According to Ibn Ḥazm, the first type is a friend whose reproach "consists of incitements and prohibitions; therein and thereby the soul is wonderfully stimulated and remarkably strengthened. . . . The second type of reproacher is the thoroughgoing scolder, who never lets up reprimanding the lover. That is a tough business, and a heavy burden to bear."[18] Nevertheless, Ibn Ḥazm explains, some men enjoy the reprimands for they provide a stern point of view against which they can rebel. The censurer was apparently an important figure in real life as well as in literature. Within the *muwashshaḥs*, he is frequently addressed with a phrase like "Stop blaming me," followed by the lover's justification for his involvement or a plea for pity. His presence adds to the dramatic quality of the poetry in the form of dialogue, intensification of the poet's feelings, and as a contrasting frame of negative chiding within which the lover can set his own positive emotions.

Tiny vignettes, revealing aspects of life in an unstable society where the Christian, Jewish, and Muslim cultures harmonized one moment and clashed the next, are also unfolded in the *muwashshaḥs*. The possibility of conversion to Islam during that period is reflected in poem No. II, by al-Aᶜmā al-Tuṭīlī, where he states that he has become a Muslim. He also wrote *muwashshaḥ* No. V, dedicated to another lad named Aḥmad, in which a conversation between the poet and a Christian tavern girl takes place. The scene delightfully presents the Christian acceptance of wine and is spiced with a pinch of picaresque humor.

> We arrived one night at a Christian tavern
> Along with guardians and night owls.

She quickly brought the wine to us
With a gracious gesture of welcome and honor
And swore by what is in the gospel:
"I have not covered it with anything but molten tar,
But it never was affected by the fire."

So I said to her, "Oh, beautiful one,
Isn't it a custom of yours to drink from the glass?"
She said, "Among us there's nothing wrong with that.
So it has been told in the reports
Of all the monks and scholars."

In *muwashshaḥ* No. 15 by Ibn ᶜUbāda, it is obvious that the Muslims of al-Andalus are aware of the Christian territory which borders their land, not to mention the monasteries and convents nestled within al-Andalus. There one encountered believers in the Holy Trinity, scornfully referred to as polytheists. The praises of al-Muᶜtaṣim were sung, Ibn ᶜUbāda comments, not as far as the eye can see, but only as far as the towns of the Christians. There were constant reminders on the horizon of the advancing threat of a rival civilization. The constant raids and battles have left their mark, too, as can be seen at the end of *muwashshaḥ* No. III, where a young girl calls out to a soldier riding off to war at night, entreating him to come to her.

Praise of rulers and important political figures also emphasizes the military atmosphere of the time. A fine maritime accent appears in No. 15, where Ibn ᶜUbāda pictures al-Muᶜtaṣim's navy in its fiery glory off the coast of Almería. The stars, which act as guides for the ships, are called upon to lead him to success and victory over the Christians. On land, lances, swords, and spears are a necessary part of the army's accouterment, and poets are apt to focus on the formations of shining armaments, comparing them to rows of glistening sharp teeth or to flashing bolts of lightning. During battle, the strength and ferocity of a lion are important attributes. For example, the Banū ᶜAbbād of Seville roar like lions in *muwashshaḥ* No. 11; and Ibn Mālik al-Saraquṣṭī calls Ibn ᶜUbayd a lion when he fights, a warrior who never turns back once he roars, in No. XXXb from *Jaish al-Tawshīḥ*. Soldiers from Muḥammad's family respond as if they were lions in the thick of battle, according to Ibn ᶜUbāda in *muwashshaḥ* No. 23.

At the same time, a truly great man would incorporate softer qualities of forgiveness, generosity, and justice into his personality. The third and fourth strophes of the bilingual *muwashshaḥ*, No. XXXV, written by the twelfth-century vizier, Ibn al-Ṣayrafī, present such a combination in a Marwānid named ᶜAbd al-Munᶜim:

Generosity, dressed in a stylish cloak of gold-embellished cloth, proudly walks

Toward ^{c}Abd al-Mun^{c}im, possessor of glory, fame, and power.
How well these traits boast of brandishing a sword of
Indian iron.
Like a thunderstorm, like a sharp saber,
like a lion,
Like a full moon that brings good luck and
has been surrounded by stars in its
splendor.

From the Marwānid family, the loftiest new moon has
lifted him to glory.
For those who are thirsty, he is water, guarded by
lions ready to spring.
How many times has he refreshed those in need with
overflowing generosity and favor.
In a timeless paradise! While blazing like
hell fire
And attacking like a lion, he lets blessings
fall like spring rain.

Similarly, a court poet praises al-Mu^{c}tamid of Seville in the Arabic *muwashshaḥ* No. 8, collected by Ibn Sanā' al-Mulk.

In him I saw the coexistence of worldly and
religious things. We are matching him
against those who preceded, and he
exceeds them.
Whoever finds fault with him is looking at
something good behind a veil.

His victory is assured by the sharp-edged spear.
He is as generous to his generation as rain clouds
are to gardens.
It's as if the mention of his name were a Koranic
verse to be recited to all mankind.
His two states consist of strength and tenderness.
So say, "Beware if he stands for war!"
And say that the clouds, if they open their palms,
do not release terror.

Since there is no separation of mosque and state in Islam, the ideal leader should manifest both spiritual and worldly characteristics. The use of water imagery to describe generosity in such men is common throughout the Middle East, for water is usually scarce in these lands and highly prized. Without it, there is no life. Just as rain brings forth new growth, so al-Mu^{c}tamid brings forth prosperity in his kingdom. In addition, the sea may also be a metaphor for unlimited generosity. The importance of mentioning a person's name as one would reiterate words from the Koran is another concept which is typically Muslim, because the Koran is believed to contain the veritable words of God, not just a translation or interpretation of God's thoughts. Each phrase, therefore, is sacred and should be repeated to all mankind. Each word and name in the awesomely beautiful text is revered and venerated. To place a ruler's name on a level with the Koran was the ultimate compliment. He may also be deemed unique, another attribute of the Koranic text. In No. 19, Ibn Baqī says of Yaḥyā ibn ᶜAlī: "Fate has decreed that you be unique and that your majesty be singular. Your excellence is evidence." Even when Ibn ᶜUbāda is praising al-Muᶜtaṣim and al-Muᶜtaḍid in the same poem, he states that both are unique among noble men. References to astrology are also made in order to indicate how highly regarded certain people are, as in No. 31, where the poet calls the Hawwarah "stars of Gemini and Aries, which are incomparable and have become proverbial." If a poet is totally in awe or has run out of metaphors of glory, he may resort to the cliché of inexpressability, declaring himself or anyone else incapable of describing the person in question. If he does attempt a physical portrayal, however, it will tend to be like those of the beloved, a kaleidoscope of full or crescent moons, willow branches, suns, lily petals, roses, and so forth, which was discussed earlier.

Besides elegant individuals and political leaders, fine wine is also praised quite frequently in these *muwashshaḥs*. Linking these two categories, al-Tuṭīlī compares a fine face with a splendid vintage wine in No. XIX. A particularly nice glimpse of wine is given by Ibn al-Labbāna in XXIX. He tells a cupbearer to hurry up and pass the wine, which resembles rays of sunshine when in the glass and, when passed in the pitcher, seems to be on fire, spinning around like a bracelet. In *muwashshaḥ* No. 23, the master craftsman Ibn ᶜUbāda has inserted a clever alphabetical play on the triliteral root which forms the word wine, *kh·m·r*:

> Go for the wine! And go early with an embroidered
> robe
> In the evening and in the morning to the music of
> the eloquent bowstring.

The name of wine, in my opinion—so know it!—is not taken
from anything but
The one who is the *khā'* of the cheek and the *mīm* of the smile
And the *rā'* of the honeyed saliva from a fragrant mouth.

> Give up worrying and join these letters
> So that you might go early and late with a body
> that has spirit.

The Arabic word for wine is *khamr*. Accordingly, cheek (*khadd*) begins with *khā'* in Arabic, smile (*mabsam*) starts with the letter, *mīm*, and saliva (*ruḍāb*) has *rā'* as its first letter. There are many plays on words stemming from the same or similar triliteral roots in this poetry, but in this case specific letters of the alphabet form part of the poem's fabric. Other examples of wine songs have already been given in Chapter III.

When it comes to imagery drawn from nature, it is hard to differentiate between spontaneous appreciation and rigid stylization. Instead of trying to distinguish a difference, it makes more sense, I believe, to assume that the original enthusiastic impulses of these Andalusian poets have been funneled through the stylistic channels open to their freely flowing emotions. Nature itself does not appear in its wild state, but as a carefully cultivated and planned garden or meadow. It is beautiful but controlled. The poets also turned to these moist flower-laden gardens when describing the human body. Their loved ones are often pictured in terms of plants, for example. Imagine relaxing in one of those shady nooks. You might look around and see bending boughs of beech and willow trees gracefully moving their dappled leaves in a soft breeze, or a small knoll not far away surrounded by fragrant flowers such as bright anemones, roses, white lilies or daisies, and emerald shoots of myrtle. Sweet basil is growing by the brook, and cherries or pomegranates ripen in the trees nearby. Generous clouds have already poured forth their rain, leaving the leaves wet and more luxuriantly green than before, just waiting for the sun to appear on the horizon. If it were evening, a moon would be expected. Birds dip here and there, and even a small garden snake might rouse itself to feed in the cool grass. Has a meadow been described, or are we just waiting for a poet's beloved to unveil her face?

Perhaps the keen awareness of color and smell which manifests itself in the *muwashshaḥs* has grown from the contemplation of such gardens. The vivid reds of roses, anemones, pomegranates, apples, and cherries are highly prized. The orange shade of turmeric is also appealing. Sharp contrasts almost always are preferred to subtle tones: black hair against white cheeks or dark green myrtle on white jasmine. Lush green is the most cherished color of all, appearing over and over again. There are green meadows after the rains, slim beloveds possess the supple movement of fresh green willow boughs. The shimmer of pearls and the glow of gold or amber also form a significant part of the poets' palette. Simultaneously, natural perfumes penetrate another level of their consciousness. Camphor is pleasing to them as well as the aroma of crushed herbs. Musk is often described in the air, along with the sweet smell of flowers, breath, or wine. Periodically these fragrances punctuate Andalusian poetry with heady accents.

The wind blowing through these sheltered spots often stirs the mind of the poet. In No. VIIb, his tears "burn in blackness like fire kindled by a moaning wind in a forsaken heart." According to Ibn Baqī in No. XII, the wind "blows weak gusts through my body and revives past sorrow, bringing me greetings from the one who torments me." Traditionally, the wind is a messenger, and is asked to carry messages to the loved ones far away. Or, as in Ibn ᶜUbāda's *muwashshaḥ* No. I, the wind may be called upon to help the lover see his beloved when they are threatened by a *raqīb*.

A poet may also wish for the freedom of a bird so that he might fly unnoticed past all obstacles guarding his beloved. Birds are often part of a *muwashshaḥ*'s imagery, portraying many different moods and symbolic functions. If the lover is feeling hamstrung and hopeless, he may be compared to a sand grouse who has been trapped in a net, or a bird without feathers trying to fly. Swooping sparrow hawks with thundering wings can stand for merciless cruelty, whereas another bird of prey, the falcon, is a symbol of nobility and honor. Conceivably, one could observe these different birds without leaving the confines of the formalized landscape.

There is hardly a stock image to be found in the first four strophes of the bilingual *muwashshaḥs* which does not have its parallel in the Arabic anthology. The abundant *topoi* continuously reappear in intricate verbal arabesques, spiraling into infinite variations of poetry and song. In this chapter, I have tried to single out the most prominent images which are shared by the Arabic and bilingual collections. Many of the same features, of course, can be found in other types of Arabic poetry, but here we are concerned only with our limited but lovely selection of *muwashshaḥs*.

CHAPTER FIVE
Differences Between the Last Stanzas

Beginning with the last strophe which leads into the *kharja*, the character of the Arabic *muwashshaḥs* collected by Ibn Sanā' al-Mulk appears to differ from that of the *muwashshaḥs* with bilingual *kharjas* preserved in the collections of Ibn Bushrā and Ibn al-Khaṭīb, despite the fact that many poems in both groups were written during the same period by the same men. Certain stylistic devices that occur frequently in the last *bait* before the bilingual *kharjas* are practically nonexistent in the *muwashshaḥs* which were written exclusively in Arabic. The most obvious variance involves the use of female voices to recite the *kharjas*. Among the bilingual *muwashshaḥs*, thirty-one of the introductory phrases feature a feminine speaker, and in two other instances the poets state that they are using the words of a girl, which makes a total of thirty-three. Yet only three out of thirty-four *kharjas* in the Arabic anthology are introduced by women. In addition to this significant discrepancy, there are certain linguistic constructions employed in the last stanza of half of the bilingual group which, with only two exceptions, do not occur in the Arabic *muwashshaḥs* in Ibn Sanā' al-Mulk's anthology. These are *rubba*, *wa rubba*, along with its shortened form, *wāw* followed by a genitive noun or adjective, and *kam*. Briefly, the first three generally mean "many a" and *kam* signifies "how many." These phrases are included in half of the bilingual *muwashshaḥs*, whereas only *wāw* with the indefinite genitive is found two times in the Arabic collection. I think it is safe to assume that, in general, where *kam*, *rubba* or *wa rubba*, and *wāw* with the indefinite genitive are used in the last *bait* of a *muwashshaḥ*, there is a stylistic reason for it. In most instances, it is probably a clue to the fact that other people are presumed to have uttered the words of the *kharjas* in addition to the figures in the poem, who are often women, according to convention. It is quite possible that these devices were used in the bilingual *muwashshaḥs* for the purpose of making it clear that the Mozarabic phrases were borrowed from popular (i.e., often repeated) lyrics. The *rubba* and *wāw* of *rubba* constructions also serve to indicate an abrupt transition within the poem, a change which quite consistently occurs in the last *bait* of the Mozarabic *muwashshaḥs*. This contrasts sharply with the Arabic poems which are less disjointed at this point and flow more smoothly through to the end.

In seven bilingual poems (Nos. IV, V, XII, XXV, XXXa, XXXIV, and XXXVI) one encounters the Arabic expression *rubba* or *wa rubba* followed by an indefinite noun or adjective in the genitive case. According to W. Wright's *Grammar of the Arabic Language*, this is the equivalent of "many a" in English. *Rubba* can also mean "perhaps," "seldom," or "once in a while," but in that case it is not followed by the genitive. De Goeje, in one of his comments concerning this usage, states:

> I do not remember ever to have seen *wa rubba* at the beginning of a sentence, nor do we ever find *rubba* employed where only a single person, object, or fact is mentioned.[1]

Although a translation of this particular form should presumably convey the idea of plurality or generalization, this has often been overlooked. I would therefore like to discuss the lines in which *rubba* occurs, keeping in mind their relationship to the *muwashshaḥ* as a whole.

In No. IV, an anonymous lovesick poet begins with a plea for affection and help from his protector. He subsequently merges this theme with a bacchic one, blaming a golden wine for causing him to reveal the secret of his love. A toast is then offered in honor of the vizier, Muḥammad, whose handsome features are described. The poet, who portrays himself as a slave in this relationship, wonders how he can hope to be united with a gazelle whose eyes are so hostile. "How many have been made captives by their flirtatiousness and languidness!" he exclaims. Their glances are capable of making men pine away. Here the last *bait* begins with many a young maiden (*rubba ʿadhrāʾa*) yearning for a meeting with her beloved; and if she sees him, she wishes to dispel his fear of the troublesome spy (*raqīb*). By simple juxtaposition instead of an explanatory transition, the poet suggests that this girl desires the same thing he does, a reunion with the beloved. The *kharja* states this in her own words. The use of *kam* (how many) in the preceding lines also makes us focus on an unknown number of victims, and it is natural to conjecture about the young maidens who might have been among them. We are prepared for this juxtaposition, and it does not jolt our ears. What may seem out of place to a modern Western reader is the sudden introduction of the spy (*raqīb*). The change from masculine to feminine has already taken place within the poem, however;

and, given the sociological context of the time, a *raqīb*'s constant chaperonage is consistent with the mention of young women. In tone, this blends well with the rest of the *muwashshaḥ*, and the shift from the specific to the general has been handled with ease.

A similar treatment can be seen in No. V, where al-Tuṭīlī describes his infatuation with Aḥmad. In the second to last strophe, he comments about the young man's piercing glances: "How many fierce lions have they killed!" Once again there is a transition from the singular to the plural which prepares the listener to hear that many a young girl (*wa rubba fatātin*) has already been treated with disdain and haughtiness by him. In this way, al-Tuṭīlī presents an example of others who have suffered because of Aḥmad. The fact that they are young women does not matter. They too fall in love with proud, handsome men and give voice to their sorrow. Other feminine *kharjas* which parallel the poets' tormented feelings are contained in *muwashshaḥs* No. XII and No. XXXVI, by Ibn Baqī and al-Khabbāz al-Mursī, respectively. In the twelfth *muwashshaḥ*, Ibn Baqī laments both harsh treatment and separation from his beloved, just as many a young woman (*wa rubba khaudin*) has sung of her grief under similar circumstances. In No. XXXVI, after the poet complains of his sleeplessness, he explains that many a beautiful woman (*rubba ḥasnā'i*) has sung of a passion like his after being deprived of sleep by her lover's absence.

In three other bilingual *muwashshaḥs* where this device appears, it is preceded by several stanzas of praise and is not as well coordinated with those verses. Many a lass (*wa rubba khaudin*) has been charmed by Abū al-Hasan and can be cured of her illness only by him in poem No. XXXa; and many a young girl (*wa rubba fatātin*) sang, complaining of the misery caused by not being able to see her beloved vizier, Ibn ᶜAbd Allāh, in No. XXXIV. Both situations involve unknown women in love with an identified man. Since this abrupt way of introducing the *kharjas* indicates another personality trait of the men being praised, namely their ability to captivate female hearts, it is not out of tune with the whole poem. Al-Tuṭīlī adopts a different procedure in No. XXV and suddenly starts talking about the beautiful women with colored fingertips (*rubba makhḍūbi al-banāni*) whom he himself has visited. The subject of the previous stanzas is dropped and not mentioned again. Except for the figure of the poet in the preceding stanza, there is no connection between the two parts of the poem. The last *bait* serves only as an introduction to the *kharja* at the end.

The shortened form of *wa rubba* with the indefinite genitive is *wāw* alone, followed by an indefinite noun or adjective in the genitive case. According to W. Wright, we often encounter the indefinite genitive alone after the conjunction, *wāw*, because of the elision of *rubba*; this *wāw* of *rubba* is equivalent in meaning to *rubba*.[2] This construction can be found in the last *bait* of seven bilingual *muwashshaḥs*, Nos. I, III, XVI, XXIV, XXVI, XXIX, and XXXVIII. There seems to be some doubt, however, concerning the translation of this elided form. According to De Goeje, "There are a great many cases where it is impossible to render it by *many a*, as it appears from the context that a single person, a single fact is recorded, so that we must translate it by *I remember*, *I think of*, *O that!* etc."[3] In conjunction with this, Andras Hamori comments that frequently the function of this *wāw* of *rubba* before singular nouns is to blur the difference between singular and plural, "and so to get at the typical through the particular."[4] Both Stern and García Gómez have chosen to translate this *wāw* with a genitive singular noun as if it pertained to one particular individual or instance: *une jeune fille*, *una moza*, *una doncella*, or *una noche*, for example. This renders the verses more immediate and the lyricism more poignant. For this reason, their translations cannot be criticized. As a stylistic element in Arabic which can indicate something about the bilingual *muwashshaḥs*, on the other hand, this construction should not be overlooked; for if one hunts for it in the last *bait* of the *muwashshaḥs* in Ibn Sanā' al-Mulk's anthology, it is almost impossible to find. In order to focus on this plural or generalized aspect of the *wāw* of *rubba*, I will incorporate the accepted meaning, "many a," in my discussion below, even though it is not necessarily the most poetic choice.

As in some of the above panegyrics, Ibn al-Labbāna and Ibn Ruḥaym, in Nos. XXIX and XXXVIII, respectively, use this phrase to introduce a young girl (*wa ghādatin* and *wa fatātin*) who has fallen in love with the man being praised, in order to have this collective figure sing the *kharja*. There is a change of subject here to which the *wāw* of *rubba* draws our attention. In al-Muᶜtamid's *muwashshaḥ* No. XXVI, the *wāw*-plus-genitive construction is combined with night (*lail*) to indicate an indefinite number of times when the words of the *kharja* might have been spoken. The theme of love in this *bait* is a continuation of what has preceded and, as a result, blends in well with the rest of the poem. The anonymous *muwashshaḥs*, Nos. XVI and XXIV, are both love poems in which this *wāw* is the first word of the last stanza. In No. XVI, a comparison is set up between the emotions of the poet and those of the women who have suffered like him, whereas in No. XXIV, the poet jumps from his own woes to a description of a situation which they call to his mind. The imagery in this *muwashshaḥ* is consistent, and the lover who is so rough with the young girl represents a problem confronted by the poet in the preceding verses. Although his imagination created the vision of serpents springing at him from the wavy locks of his beloved's temples, the poet makes us realize that his psychic pain is no less real than her physical suffering. In poems No. I by Ibn ᶜUbāda and No. III by an unknown author, the emotional tenor is maintained by presenting circumstances that reflect the poet's lovelorn state, despite the lack of a logical connection between the main part of the *muwashshaḥ* and the last introductory *bait*. Both use the phrase, many a young woman (*wa ghādatin*), leading into the *kharja*.

There are only two places where this *wāw* of *rubba* appears in the last *bait* of a *muwashshaḥ* in Ibn Sanā' al-Mulk's Arabic anthology. In No. 15, where Ibn ᶜUbāda extols al-Muᶜtaṣim of Almería, many festivals (*wa mahrajānin*) are mentioned in the lines leading up to the *kharja* that begins with the exclamation, "What a wonderful festival this is!" This gives an impression of a continuous state of joy and well-being in the kingdom rather than an isolated day or incident. *Muwashshaḥ* No. 13, possibly by Ibn al-Labbāna, is the second one where this construction appears in the last *bait*. Because of the context, its generalized aspect can best be translated here as "sometimes." In this poem, the *wāw* of *rubba* marks an abrupt transition, for the last *bait* has no relation to the preceding part of the *muwashshaḥ*, where the poet portrays himself wasting away from unrequited love. Its main function is to introduce a saucy *kharja*. To appreciate the brusque transition, let's look at the end of the poem:

> Are you going to reprimand me?
> Or will you have mercy and prevent the wasting away of the one in love if he becomes ill with grief?
> Woe unto me! I am imprisoned in a sea of fears whose shore is far away. I can only cling to the waves.
>
> Sometimes a young girl appears like the full moon rising.
> What a breast on a branch of laurel!
> Her leaves are a garment more red than the rose.
> She spent the night while singing,
> "My darling, make up your mind. Arise! Hurry and kiss my mouth. Come embrace
> My breast and raise my anklets to my earrings. My husband is busy."

The last *bait* clarifies nothing about the poet's state of anxiety or the beloved, Aḥmad, nor does it provide a parallel situation, as in some *muwashshaḥs* in the bilingual collection. A tart, startling ending is characteristic of the *muwashshaḥ*; but it is significant that in the only instance where *wāw* is combined with young women (*ghādatin*) in the Arabic anthology, it is not as well woven into the fabric of the whole poem as are the examples cited from the bilingual group. It seems that the form rather than the essence of the Mozarabic versions has been imitated here.

An analogous exclamation which occurs seven times in the last *bait* of the bilingual collection (Nos. VI, XIV, XVII, XXVI, XXXb, XXXI, XXXV, and XXXVII) is *kam*, "how many" or "how much," a phrase which is not found in the last *bait* of any *muwashshaḥ* in the Arabic anthology. *Kam* is also a quantative expression which colors the context in which the *kharja* is set. In all but No. XXVI, such phrases as "how many complained" and "how many found no sleep during his absence," in which feminine subjects are indicated by the use of feminine verbal endings, or "how many young girls say to their mother" and "how many tender young maidens sang" convey the impression that the situations are common ones, shared by many. A second implication is that the ensuing *kharjas*, or at least their lyrical motifs, have been repeated often, usually by young women. The only two exceptions to the use of a female voice in conjunction with these expressions are encountered in No. 15 from Ibn Sanā' al-Mulk's series, where a presumably male servant exclaims the *kharja*, and in No. XXVI, from Ibn Bushrā's collection, where the *kharja* is sung by the poet himself.

These stylistic devices automatically transfer the *kharja* and the experience of the people singing them to a general plane. It is no longer a uniquely personal body of lyrical poetry. We are told in an indirect manner that many others have uttered these words before. The *kharja* must thus become at once more universal and impersonal despite its poignant emotional content. A tension is created between the antecedent individualized expression and the words of the *kharja* which have been shared by many in the past. If indeed the *kharjas* were known by most people living then, if they were a part of a common popular culture, there would have been an additional element of suspense added when the singer exclaimed, "How many lasses sang in grief!" The audience would have been guessing which one of their favourite songs it might be. If the listeners were not familiar with the short lyrics of the *kharja*, there would have been a delightful surprise and dramatic change of linguistic structure in these last lines, the focal point of the whole poem.

In the bilingual group of *muwashshaḥs*, the expressions *kam*, *rubba*, and the *wāw* of *rubba* each appear seven times. This adds up to twenty-one and represents half of the total. Out of thirty-four Arabic *muwashshaḥs*, the more elusive *wāw* of *rubba* appears, as we saw, only twice. This seems to indicate that a high percentage of the *kharjas* with Romance words in them may be of a more popular and general nature than the Arabic ones included in *Dār al-Ṭirāz*. As we have noticed, in the case of both *kam* and *rubba* followed by a genitive, a plural is definitely indicated; and, although the exact interpretation of the *wāw* with a genitive cannot be so easily specified, it does seem to imply something typical if not a concrete plural. Perhaps the authors of the bilingual *muwashshaḥs* wished to state in this subtle way that their *kharjas* belonged to the public domain. These stylistic components suggest that at least half of the bilingual *kharjas* have probably been sung before.

This is also true of the Arabic *muwashshaḥ* No. 13, whose anonymous author chose an erotic cliché as a finale. The proof of its diffusion has been cited by García Gómez in his notes about the Mozarabic *kharja* at the end of *muwashshaḥ* No. IX, which is very similar, although it does not mention the absent husband: "I will not love you unless you join my anklet to my earring." He has previously documented this erotic passage with reference to classical Arabic verse and has also found another *kharja* like it in *Jaish al-Tawshīḥ*, which is entirely in Arabic: "Lift my anklet to my earrings. My husband is busy."[5]

This duplicates part of *muwashshaḥ* No. 13's *kharja* almost word for word. On the other hand, the above observations about the *wāw* of *rubba* do not apply to the last stanza of *muwashshaḥ* No. 15. Despite the fact that Ibn ᶜUbāda may have used the phrase, "many a festival," to round out the picture of a happy, satisfied kingdom, thereby giving the impression that a servant might utter such a *kharja* at almost any time, the style is literary rather than colloquial, and it is written with desinential inflection (*iᶜrāb*), which was not used in colloquial speech. It is undoubtedly a unique *kharja*, composed by Ibn ᶜUbāda for this particular occasion. Furthermore, this poem lacks the abrupt shift from a masculine voice to that of a female in the last stanza, a feature which is normally present in the *muwashshaḥs* which contain these generalizing elements.[6]

All of the Mozarabic *kharjas* are written in the colloquial language of the Christians and Jews living under Muslim rulers, a Romance dialect mixed with a great many Arabic words. The verses also contain now archaic elements which, due to our lack of information about that language, cannot be attributed with any degree of certitude either to regional isolation or to the fact that these short poems are much older than their authors. Yet we do have concrete evidence that a number of the *muwashshaḥs* cited above contain *kharjas* used elsewhere. The *kharjas* of Nos. XII, XVIII, XXII, XXVIII, and XXXVIII have survived as appendages to Hebrew *muwashshaḥs*, while Nos, VII, XXI, and XXX end with *kharjas* that have been duplicated in other Arabic texts. Given the paucity of extant manuscripts, one might suppose that others were used again and again, too. This will have to suffice as proof for the moment of the high esteem in which they were held in al-Andalus. Obviously they were well liked. Other poets appreciated certain *kharjas* enough to borrow them as endings for their own *muwashshaḥs*. This does not prove that they took them from an earlier written manuscript, from traditional unwritten songs being sung by the people of al-Andalus, or from another *muwashshaḥ* which they might have heard in a sophisticated court setting.

Certain *kharjas* seem to be more traditional in nature than others. In the case of al-Tuṭīlī's *kharja* No. XXV, close parallels were found by García Gómez in the lyrics of Lope de Vega, who lived centuries later. García Gómez thinks that this *kharja* existed before the *muwashshaḥ* was composed and that it stems from a Romance tradition celebrating the night of St. John (June 23 or 24).[7] Here we have a theme from the Middle Ages which appears again during the Golden Age. It probably never died, but continued in versions sung by the populace or in the courts for generations. This hypothesis is substantiated by S. G. Armistead and J. H. Silverman, who encountered other variations of the same theme in several collections of Spanish *romances* from different parts of the Iberian peninsula, along with a sample preserved by the descendants of Spanish Jews in Morocco.[8] Continuing this line of thought, James Monroe concludes that al-Tuṭīlī must have adapted the first two verses of a Romance ballad to fit the canons of Arabic rhyme and meter. He reconstructs the hypothetical Romance model with octosyllabic verses and assonant *a – a* rhyme, and he shows how the poet could have Arabized the couplet to achieve the necessary consonant rhyme (*-qā*) and an acceptable meter (*ramal* dimeter) which coincides with the syllable count and stress patterns of the original Romance octosyllable.[9] Not all *kharjas* follow such recognized patterns, but this type of research corroborates my belief that the stylistic devices chosen by the poets to introduce the *kharjas* should not be ignored. Their ability to universalize and typify is convincing.

In studying these last stanzas leading into the *kharjas*, another contrast between the two groups immediately stands out. In thirty-one of the bilingual *muwashshaḥs*, women sing the *kharja*; in two others, the poet indicates that the speaker is using the words of a girl; and in a third, the author speaks but addresses his mother just like a young girl. This makes a total of thirty-four, or 75 percent of the whole. In the Arabic collection, only three *kharjas* are attributed to a female, which amounts to only 9 percent. Here we are confronting an extrinsic feminine aspect of the *muwashshaḥ* and find that there is a great difference between the two collections. It may be just a literary convention to attribute the *kharja* to a female voice, but such conventions cannot be dismissed lightly. In Arabic poetry, for example, poets traditionally refer to the beloved with the personal pronouns, *huwa* and *hu*, which are masculine. This does not eliminate the use of feminine pronouns, for they are often found, especially where names are given. But before a feminine name appears, the masculine pronoun is employed. This generality applies equally to the main body of *muwashshaḥs* in both groups, although a difference arises when it comes to the last *bait*. In most poems in the Arabic anthology compiled by Ibn Sanā' al-Mulk, the poets continue using this conventional masculine wording, either in reference to themselves as the first person, or for a second or third person. In the majority of bilingual poems, the authors shift from masculine pronouns to feminine ones, from their own masculine voice to that of a woman, in the last *bait*. An abrupt change is made which cannot be explained in terms of the *muwashshaḥ*'s context. There is no internal rationale unless one examines the Mozarabic *kharja* and its intrinsic feminine characteristics, which will be done in the next chapter. On an external basis, one has to look for another literary convention, one which would undoubtedly be alien to the classical Eastern Arabic manner. Under the circumstances, this could have come from Romance, or European, poetry and song. Too many parallels have been found in French, Provençal, Portuguese, and German for us to doubt that such a tradition existed during the Middle Ages in Europe. The possibility of North African models should not be discounted either. None, however, have been discovered to be earlier than the Andalusian *kharjas*.

In the theoretical discussion of the *muwashshaḥ*, Ibn Sanā' al-Mulk does not stress the feminine voice. All he says is that the *kharja* must be introduced by animate, inanimate, or abstract beings, using such verbs as "sing" or "say." There is no emphasis on femininity, which is true of his anthology also. Those of us who are familiar with the *muwashshaḥs* in the collection compiled by García Gómez and have seen the Mozarabic *kharjas* in books and articles by Stern, Cantera, Dámaso Alonso, Heger, and Solá-Solé, to mention only a few, tend to take the feminine element for granted in these bilingual poems. Since Romance verses undoubtedly were not understood by the Egyptian compiler, he could not have made use of them even though he might have had access to *muwashshaḥs* in which they were included. We cannot help but notice that he left the Mozarabic dialect out of his work and that there is a scarcity of female voices in his anthology, where young women are introduced only three times. The masculine voice of the poet, a servant, or the abstract personality of glory or battle appear instead. In fact, there are twice as many places in Ibn Sanā' al-Mulk's anthology where metaphorical speakers occur than in the bilingual corpus. In the latter group, the heart, war, and glory each introduce one *kharja*, whereas in the former group of Arabic *muwashshaḥs*, there are six metaphorical speakers: glory, doves, longing, passion, battle, and the emirate. Furthermore, other human figures besides the poet, a girl, or the beloved sing *kharjas* in the Arabic anthology. The poet may bring in a group leader or a servant to recite the final verses, a phenomenon which does not occur in the bilingual *muwashshaḥs* that are extant.

Far more prevalent than either a girl or a metaphorical agent in the Arabic series' introductions to the *kharja* is the voice of the masculine poet himself, employing the verbs, "I said," "I sang," and so forth. Nineteen of the Arabic kharjas are clearly presented by the author. Only seven are uttered by the poet in the collection of Mozarabic *muwashshaḥs*; and, as briefly mentioned above, in one of these instances (No. XIII) he claims that he is singing just like a young girl, while in another (No. XXXIII) he very inappropriately addresses his mother, which leads me to think that he should have attributed the *kharja* to a girl.

Female speakers are not unknown in classical Arabic poetry, but the frequency with which women appear at the very end of poems like the bilingual *muwashshaḥs* to sing verses which are so strongly feminine in character is unusual. The difference, then, between the number of female voices in each linguistic group may very possibly be due to two separate literary traditions which, in turn, have evolved from distinct cultural atmospheres.[10] Perhaps the young Mozarab girl with her particular type of song, almost like a characteristic epithet, became fashionable for a period of time in Andalusian literary circles. Why she was typically depicted in this way we do not know. Were educated men who were interested in the ways of the people responsible for this initially? Was it a result of adapting existing songs of the indigenous population or an invention on the part of a bilingual poet? Once again these questions must be asked. In the next chapter about the *kharjas* themselves, this problem will be approached from another perspective. Meanwhile, I hope that the above facts have indicated that there are significant discrepancies between the final strophes of the *muwashshaḥs* which contain colloquial Romance words and phrases, as presented in the texts of Ibn Bushrā and Ibn al-Khaṭīb, and those composed totally in Arabic which Ibn Sanā al-Mulk collected.

CHAPTER SIX
Arabic and Mozarabic *Kharjas*

If Ibn Sanā al-Mulk had read only the bilingual *muwashshaḥs* found in the manuscripts of Ibn al-Khaṭīb and Ibn Bushrā, I think that he would have written the part of his theoretical treatise which deals with the *kharja* quite differently. To begin with, he probably would have indicated that the majority of *kharjas* should be introduced by women and that the content should express a female point of view. This is a rather radical break with the classical Arabic tradition which poets generally follow in the main part of the *muwashshaḥs*. In addition, the mother figure, who is never even mentioned by Ibn Sanā' al-Mulk, would have been singled out by him as a person to whom a young girl would appropriately address her questions and laments when not speaking directly to the beloved *ḥabīb*. Concerning formulas of style, he undoubtedly would have noted that the girl often asks a question like "what will I do?" and that her phrases are apt to be repetitious, a characteristic which clashes with the rules of Arabic poetics. Furthermore, he would have excluded all categories except love lyrics in the *kharjas*. Not one of the *kharjas* with Romance words deviates from the theme of love, whereas a third of the Arabic *kharjas* feature panegyrics or, less often, asceticism. This, in turn, would eliminate the need for desinential inflection (*iʿrāb*) when praising particular men in the *kharja*. For that matter, the question of desinential inflection in regard to Romance vernacular is irrelevant. Thus the evidence builds up, point by point, indicating that there are discrepancies between the *muwashshaḥs* with bilingual Mozarabic *kharjas* and those solely in Arabic.

Perhaps the most readily noticeable difference is the feminine quality of so many Mozarabic *kharjas*, which can hardly be found in Ibn Sanā' al-Mulk's anthology. Besides the contrast between the number of female introductory voices which frame the *kharjas* of both series, the majority of *kharjas* with

Romance words contain intrinsic feminine elements which would indicate that a young girl or woman was speaking, even if she had not been mentioned in the *bait* beforehand. Thirty-one *kharjas* out of a total of thirty-eight in the collections of Ibn Bushrā and Ibn al-Khaṭīb are basically feminine, whereas only three or four can be found in the thirty-four *muwashshaḥs* in *Dār al-Ṭirāz* which reflect a woman's attitude. Since masculine pronouns may refer to either men or women, the problem of homosexual as well as heterosexual love arises. I would therefore like to specify which elements I feel are essentially feminine. Only the words of the *kharjas* themselves will be considered, without reference to the phrases that introduced them.

First of all, in eleven Mozarabic *kharjas* (Nos. VI, X, XIV, XV, XVII, XIX, XXI, XXX, XXXI, XXXIII, and XXXIV) a young girl addresses her mother, something which does not happen even once in *Dār al-Ṭirāz*.[1] She is often distressed and asking her mother what to do about an unhappy situation, or complaining that she cannot sleep; but in the Arabic anthology, where the poets frequently fret about similar problems, complaints are not addressed to a mother figure. Nevertheless, it is a perfectly natural reaction for a girl to take her mother into her confidence (or another woman, perhaps a Celestina-type, whom she might call mother) under such circumstances.

The total absence of this motif in Ibn Sanā' al-Mulk's collection is striking. It may merely indicate, however, that he did not choose to include Arabic examples of this type because it is so alien to the classical literary traditions with which he was familiar. Furthermore, according to S. M. Stern, poets like Ibn Sanā' al-Mulk gradually replaced the original Andalusian models with their own versions of the genre.

> As the *muwashshaḥs* of the more important Oriental *washshāḥūn* acquired the status of classics, littérateurs began to care less about the Western poems. This state of affairs thus contrasts sharply with what happened in North Africa, where the *muwashshaḥ* was less cultivated independently, and in consequence the Andalusian *muwashshaḥ* as such took a much faster hold.[2]

The difference between Eastern and Western literary tastes may at least partially account for the omission of the mother-daughter theme in *Dār al-Ṭirāz*. In contrast, the Andalusian author, Ibn al-Khaṭīb included the following Arabic *kharja* in *Jaish al-Tawshīḥ*:

hākadhā yā umm nashqā	Thus, O mother, am I made miserable,
wa-l-ḥabīb sākin jiwārī	While my lover dwells in my neighborhood.
in amut yā qawm ᶜīshqā	If I die, O people, of love,
fa-khudū ummī bi-thāṛī	Then exact my bloodwit from him, mother.[3]

Given the existence of *kharjas* like this in Arabic, it is quite plausible that Ibn Sanā' al-Mulk may have overlooked a poetic tradition, shared by people speaking both Arabic and Romance in the Maghrib, when he was making his selection.

Portraits of a young girl with her mother also appear in the literature of other cultures and periods, as Theodore Frings and Peter Dronke have proven.[4] Within the geographical boundaries of the Arabic-speaking world, this type of mother-daughter relationship is contained in ancient Egyptian poetry and, according to James Monroe, may be found in the popular Ḥawfī poetry of North Africa. In classical Arabic poetry of the pre-Islamic period and early centuries of Islam, it does not seem to have been represented, even though conversations about love with sisters, friends, or female slaves have been recorded. The following three excerpts from the *Diwān* of ᶜUmar ibn Abī Rabīᶜah (d. ca. 719) illustrate this point. Two have been translated into English and the other into French. The italics used are mine.

1. "They let her know" said ᶜOmar, "that I was married, she concealed her anger silently.

"Then she said to her sister and another person: I wish he had married ten.

"But to *other women* with whom she withdrew her veil, she said:

"Why does my heart appear to be not a part of me and why do my bones feel weak?

"Just because of the horrible news which has been brought to me, which burned, so that I felt there were hot coals in my heart."[5]

2. "She let the tent flap fall and said: Do not care about *my family*; talk to me!

"We kept chatting to each other to the exclusion of her *woman attendants* who knew well what an anguished lover desires.

"They were aware of what she wanted and said to her: Allow us to go walking in the plain for an hour to enjoy the fresh night.

"She said: Do not stay long! They replied: Continue talking, we shall soon join in again; and like gazelles of the sand slipped away.

"And when they arose they let every intelligent person know that what they were doing was just for my sake."[6]

3. *Toutes les trois* ensemble
parlerent de moi
lorsque j'apparaissais
la première disait: "Le connaissez-vous?"
La seconde répondait:
"Mais oui, c'est ᶜOmar."
La troisième qui était ma préférée

> répliquait: "Nous le connaissons
> comment peut-on donc cacher la lune?"[7]

Even Ibn Ḥazm in his autobiographical comments in *The Ring of the Dove* does not mention his own mother. Using plural forms, he tells how he was raised in al-Andalus by women. Whether this stems from a reluctance to mention female members of the family by name or from the aristocratic Muslim family structure itself, where a number of women must have shared the raising of children in the women's quarters of the home, I am not sure. Whatever the reason, the mother is not a central figure in classical Arabic literature, whereas she is found in colloquial North African poems and has become an important part of traditional Hispanic poetry over the centuries, as Menéndez Pidal has shown.[8] Whether or not the mother-daughter relationship antecedes the *kharjas* as a literary theme in Romance or Arabic dialects one can only conjecture, for there is no extant vernacular poetry in either language which antedates the *kharjas.*[9]

Except for explanatory references to the *kharja* in the last stanza, where the poets explain in Arabic that a girl is going to speak to her mother (*umm*), all but two of the words for mother in the bilingual *kharjas* are in Romance. *Mammā* is the one used in eight cases, with *maṭre* as an alternate form. The fact that poets shift from the Arabic, *umm*, in the last *bait* to *mammā* in the *kharja* in seven *muwashshaḥs* indicates to me that they are attempting to reproduce the speech of a native Andalusian girl who speaks the Mozarabic dialect. Although there is no way of telling whether she is a Christian, Jew, or a convert to Islam, it does seem realistic to assume that the family structure to which she is accustomed is different from that found in an aristocratic Muslim home, as reflected in literature. Her family appears to be more nuclear, with a close relationship between mother and daughter. The daughter depends upon her mother for advice and consolation. Although I do not know what role poetic imagination has played in creating this relationship, I assume that it must be based to some extent on social reality because it would have been easy to depict the girl talking to another woman. Additional evidence is furnished by the use of Arabic words for the beloved, like *ḥabīb* and *sīdī* (my lord). Why couldn't the girl use the Arabic word, *umm*, for her mother in most instances? I believe that in daily life *mammā* must have been used along with *ḥabīb*. Within a Mozarab family, the girls probably grew up calling her mother either *mammā* or *maṭre*; but living in territory taken over by people speaking Arabic, she would have called an Arabic-speaking lover, *ḥabīb*. According to Ibn Khaldūn, "the dialects of the urban population follow the language of the nation or race that has control of (the cities in question) or has founded them."[10] Basic words such as father or mother would undoubtedly be among the last to change in a conquered people's language.

The spy or *raqīb* is another character involved in a young woman's life who appears in the Mozarabic *kharjas*.[11] Appointed to watch her, a *raqīb* is able to thwart her freedom. A guarded woman, therefore, must plan her actions around his movements, arranging to meet her beloved when the *raqīb* is not there. *Kharja* No. IV illustrates such a situation, and its feminine nature seems obvious to me. *Kharja* No. XXVIII, on the other hand, is puzzling. In both version a and b, the *kharja* seems to represent homosexual love rather than a bond between man and woman. The speaker, who is the poet himself in each *muwashshaḥ*, says that he has loved a *filyol aleyno* (someone else's child) whose *raqīb* now wants to separate them:

> I loved someone else's child and he loved me.
> His *raqīb* wants to take him away from me.

There are several different transcriptions of this *kharja*,[12] but the words being questioned here, *filyol aleyno* and *raqīb*, seem to be quite consistent throughout the different versions. As the *kharja* has been interpreted, the only Arabic word is *raqīb*. Is it possible that the poet used the verses of a Mozarab girl to express his love? She might easily have referred to an Arabic-speaking boy as *filyol aleyno*, and the type of *raqīb* mentioned may be one of those irritating creatures described by Ibn Ḥazm who spies on both men and women, trying to cause trouble and break up a romance:

> Then there is the spy who has discovered an inkling of what the loving pair are about, and has some suspicion of what is going on; he desired to ferret out the whole truth of the case, and therefore hangs about and squats for hours on end, watching their movements, eyeing their expressions, counting their very breaths. Such a man is more pestilential than the mange.[13]

This hypothesis may not be too far fetched, for the following *muwashshaḥs* end with a *kharja* which contains the speech of a Mozarab girl in love with a young man: No. I, addressed to Abū ᶜAmr, No. III, sung to a young soldier, No. XIV, written for Aḥmad, No. XXXVI, created for ᶜĪsa, No. XVI for Faraj, and No. XXXII for another young man. In the case of No. XXVIIIa and XXVIIIb, we cannot be certain of the beloved's sex, but the *kharja* does suggest that both poets may have been following a vogue and using the plaint of a Mozarab girl as an ending for the poem. They have not bothered with any transition, though, and the result is confusing. To resolve this question, I would like to turn to a *muwashshaḥ* by the Hebrew poet, Ibn Ezra, who introduces the identical *kharja* as follows:

> My heart was broken by an eloquent doe who, recalling to mind that someone treacherously divides those who are bound together, sang before me, weeping, a song of the gazelles.[14]

Unlike the Arab poets, Ibn Baqī and Ibn Mālik al-Saraqusṭī, who used this *kharja*, Ibn Ezra removes our doubts about the speaker. Through his choice of a doe as the central figure here, he makes it clear that this *kharja* is the song of a young woman who is worried about the *raqīb*'s malevolent intent.

A third kind of intrinsically feminine *kharja* is the complaint about a rough or careless lover, as seen in Mozarabic *kharjas* Nos. XXII, XXIV, and X, or in No. 27 from Ibn Sanā' al-Mulk's Arabic collection. In No. XXII, the girl cries out, startled:

> Don't bite me, oh, beloved. No!
> I don't like rough treatment.
> The tunic is fragile. That's enough!
> I don't want any part of this.

Her lover's brusque advances have overwhelmed her and she wants to be left alone. In No. X, the protest is heard by the mother rather than the lover, but the essential quality is similar. Here, after telling her mother that a shameless man has taken her by force, she indicates her apprehensiveness about the future and what will become of her. It is improbable that a man would be so concerned. This is true of the Arabic *kharja*, No. 27, also:

> Alas! What has happened to me! I dallied with him, and
> he ruined my dress and my locks of hair!

Even more serious consequences are mentioned in Nos. XXVII and XXXI, where the threat of death hangs over the young woman and her lover. In *kharja* No. XXVII, her affair has been discovered and she fears for her own life, while in No. XXXI, it is her lover who would be exposed to death if they are seen. Both *kharjas* end with the bewildered girl's anxious plea, "what shall I do?"

The very sensual reference to making love in *kharja* No. IX from Ibn Bushrā's text and in No. 13 from *Dār al-Ṭirāz*, discussed in Chapter IV, is clearly meant to convey a certain type of woman's thinking, even if written by a man. In the bilingual *kharja* No. IX, the vocabulary, except for *non t'amarey*, is all Arabic. This fact, along with the existence of such a theme in classical Arabic literature, suggests that these verses probably stem from Middle Eastern sources. The unabashed lewdness may not seem very feminine to a modern reader, but undoubtedly literature which portrays women in such a light has always existed. In fact, the roots of this orgiastic tradition may extend back to ancient pagan ceremonies.[15] The important factor here is that the remark could only have been made by a female.

There are a number of *kharjas* in which men are mentioned or directly addressed and others in which *ḥabīb* (darling or beloved) appears. Because *ḥabīb* can refer to either a man or a woman, only the context indicates the difference. Therefore, I do not consider the presence of *ḥabīb* to be sufficient evidence of a *kharja*'s feminine nature. Nouns like *sīdī* (my lord) in colloquial

Arabic, *filiyolo* (son) in the Mozarabic dialect, and *khil*(*l*)*ello* (friend),[16] which mixes an Arabic noun with a diminutive Romance ending, refer with little room for doubt to men. The adjective, *bono* (*bueno*, good) in *muwashshaḥ* No. XI is also clearly masculine. I believe it is correct to attribute these verses to women unless there is some indication or proof of another origin. If this point of view is accepted, then several *kharjas* should be added to the group with intrinsic feminine qualities: Nos. I, III, XI, XIII, XVIII, and XX. (No. XXVII probably falls into this category also, but it has already been discussed.) In Nos. I, III, XI, XVIII, and XX, a woman directly addresses the man rather than mentioning him indirectly to someone else. If the reading of *kharja* No. XII is considered valid, then another pair of feminine verses should be included. Since the Arabic rhyme is *-lī* instead of *-lā* throughout the *qufls*, I see no reason to doubt García Gómez's vocalized transcription, *elle*, the equivalent of *él* (he), in the *kharja*. Only if the Arabic rhyme had been *-lā* could one legitimately read the pronoun as *ella* (she).

Some of the *kharjas* reflect the cloistered life of women within the social structure. In Muslim Spain, as is traditionally the case in most cultures, it was the man who boasted of visiting women. Men played an active role, and the successful Arab adventurers were proud of slipping past guards and not being caught. Eight of the bilingual Mozarabic *kharjas* and one of the three Arabic *kharjas* introduced by a woman pertain to a lover coming to the person speaking: Nos. I, III, IV, VII, VIII, XXIII, XXXV, XXXVI, and No. 16 from the Arabic anthology. All of these *kharjas*, except for No. VIII, are specifically attributed to women in the last stanza. *Kharja* No. VIII is voiced by the poet's beloved who is a female, I presume, for there is nothing to indicate that a man is involved. The *kharja* of No. VIIa, it should be noted, is assigned to glory, but version VIIb is sung by a girl. Although the attribution of these verses to women is an extrinsic factor, it is an amazingly consistent one which reveals how basically feminine the content was thought to be.

At least one significant deviation might have been encountered to indicate the opposite situation, but none of the above-mentioned *kharjas* were attributed to males. The first Mozarabic *kharja*, taken from Ibn Bushrā's manuscript, might be cited as an exception; but I think that the *kharja* would not be as convincing if the customary relationship were not taken for granted.

> My lord, Ibrāhīm, oh, sweet name, come to me at night.
> If not, if you do not want to, I'll go to you. Tell me
> where to see you.

The girl wants to see her lover so badly that if he refuses to come to her, she will be bold enough to go to him. This defiance of the expected norm gives the *kharja* its impact. A woman is more likely to tell her lover when to come to her, as in No. III, where she calls to a soldier passing by:

Oh, lad, oh, lad
Enter here
When the jealous one is sleeping.[17]

Whoever sings *kharja* No. XXXV is taking no chances. She makes doubly sure that her message is understood, speaking first in the local Romance dialect, Mozarabic, and then inviting him in Arabic to join her. There is an element of boldness in many of these verses and at times a flirtatious, teasing manner, which can be seen in No. XI:

If you love me like a good man,
Then kiss this string of pearls,
This little mouth of cherries!

On the basis of the above analysis, twenty-nine of the thirty-eight Mozarabic *kharjas* can be categorized as intrinsically feminine. Only three of the thirty-four Arabic *kharjas* have been included so far in this category. A fourth one to consider is Ibn ʿUbāda's *kharja*, No. 9, where an example of typically feminine coyness is expressed:

I say, by God, you will never taste the sugarplum!

Two other *kharjas* in the Arabic anthology could have been voiced by women, but the chances are equally good that a man would have said them. In No. 4, this song is quoted:

My darling, you are my neighbor, your house is next
to mine, yet you are avoiding me.

The author of No. 10, who may be Ibn Baqī, exclaims:

My beloved has left me. When will I be with him again?

If these are to be interpreted as feminine lyrics exclusively, then the grief-stricken cry, "Don't leave me!" in Mozarabic *kharja* No. XXXVIII would also have to be included in this category. It would be a mistake, however, to attribute thoughts like these to a woman's psyche only.

The preponderance of feminine lyrics in the Mozarabic *kharjas* compared to the sparse scattering of such verses in the Arabic collection raises questions which I cannot even hope to answer at this moment. Is the Mozarab girl a new topic that was introduced to Arabic poetry in al-Andalus? Were her verses inspired by popular songs which already existed? Or were her words quoted verbatim from such lyrics? How many people today would like to have textual evidence in hand to confirm their answers to these questions! Did she appeal to the Arabic-speaking people as a curiosity, talking to her mother, as an amusing second-class addition, or as an excuse to add spice to the tired metaphors and stock images of the main part of the *muwashshaḥ*? Perhaps the poignancy of the lyrics was fully understood and taken to heart with a deep appreciation. I do not imagine that the poets found her phrases like *yā mammā* or *¿ké farey?* natural in Arabic verse. Because there are certain correlations between language and culture, between the way one thinks with patterns of words and the way one acts that make expressions in one language sound strange when translated into another tongue, her Mozarabic phrases must have been left intact. Being bilingual, the poets could move with ease from one language to another. Following their innate intuition, they would have written verses in whichever language was the most appropriate. The audience was bilingual, too, so comprehension would not have been a problem. But why wasn't the whole *muwashshaḥ*, whose meter and rhyme are based on the *kharja*, written from a feminine point of view to concur with the *kharja* thematically as well? Why is there an abrupt shift in these *muwashshaḥs* from a man's conception of love in the main part of the poem to a woman's outlook at the end? Perhaps A. B. Lord's comment about epic poetry can be applied to lyrical poetry as well. He states that "the songs of Christian groups will have themes and formulas distinctive from those of Moslem groups, and *vice versa*."[18] If so, the reason for this change might be explained by the influence of an alien literary tradition or by daily contact with another culture. Whether or not these women's songs are Christian or pre-Christian is not as important as the fact that they seem to spring from a non-Muslim source which existed in the Iberian peninsula.[19]

Another well-documented feature of epic poetry which should be considered in relation to the Mozarabic lyrics is the formulaic oral nature of the phrases which are repeated so consistently. Scholars like Menéndez Pidal and Margit Frenk Alatorre have commented on the frequency with which questions such as *¿ké farey?* are asked by these young women.[20] I would like to document the questions found in the bilingual *kharjas* taken from Ibn Bushrā and Ibn al-Khaṭīb and compare them with the few that occur in the *kharjas* of Ibn Sanā' al-Mulk's anthology. In five Mozarabic *kharjas*, the above-mentioned query appears:

No. VI: ¿Ké farey, yā ummī?
No. XXI: Gar ké fareyo, yā mammā.
No. XXVII: ¿Ké farey?
No. XXXI: Mammā, gar ké faray.
No. XXXVIII: ¿Ké fareyo o ké serad de mibe?

Here we are confronted with a formulaic expression which must have belonged to an oral tradition. According to A. B. Lord, an expression becomes a formula if a poet uses it many times. Then if it is used by other poets, it enters the tradition and becomes a traditional formula. "All this is within the realm of oral composition on the formula level," he explains.[21] Further research in this area would be fruitful, for the oral traditional aspect of the Mozarabic *kharjas* and their relation to comparable Romance lyrics have yet to be thoroughly studied. This is just one example that bears evidence of an established tradition of Romance lyrics of an unwritten oral nature.

In *Dār al-Ṭirāz*, this question is nowhere to be found. The closest the Arabic *kharjas* come to this can be seen in the following two examples.

> My beloved has left me. When will I be with him again?

This *kharja*, from *muwashshaḥ* No. 10, ends with a rhetorical question which is more like a sigh. The second one, from No. 20, contains a question addressed to an unknown beloved on whom the burden of responsibility is placed:

> What a long night without a single helper!
> Oh, heart of someone, can't you be assuaged?

Questions within this Arabic anthology are not repeated verbatim, and their content does not set them off so readily from the rest of the poem.

Underlying the Mozarab girl's repeated wail, "what shall I do?" there may be an unconscious cultural attitude. She is obviously distraught, but her choice of words indicates that she is not passively resigned. Her searching contrasts with the fatalistic attitude expressed in the Arabic *kharja*, No. 29:

> Fate has decided on separation, oh, ᶜAbd al-Ḥaqq,
> So desire does not allow me to live and leaves me
> nothing.

Although this is a cliché, it succinctly represents a traditional Muslim belief in the power of God's absolute will, which controls the world minute by minute in continuous and foreordained creation. The young Mozarab girl, in contrast, often wonders what to do. She may be tearful, trembling, and very young, yet her plaint often takes the form of a question about her predicament. She may be concerned about her beloved's behavior or her own feelings and response. In the *kharja* of *muwashshaḥ* No. II, she wants to know how to bear her lover's absence, and in No. XXXVII another girl asks why her lover will not give her his "medicine." Again a question arises in *kharja* No. V: "Tell me why do you wish—oh, God!—to kill me?" The interrogative, *por qué* (why), seems to imply a cultural acceptance of the principle of cause and effect. The use of the first person as an active, inquiring agent is not found in the *kharjas* of *Dār al-Ṭirāz*.

Simple repetition is another form of expression which occurs often in the Mozarabic lyrics. "Oh, lad, oh, lad," a girl calls out to a soldier in *kharja* No. III, while the exclamation, "mercy, mercy, oh, handsome one," is combined with a parallel form of address, "oh, God," in *kharja* No. V. In No. XXI, the words, "oh, Mama," open the *kharja*, with Mama repeated emphatically at the end of the third line.

Oh, Mama, my beloved
Is going and will not return again.
Tell me what shall I do, Mama.
Won't he leave me a little kiss?[22]

A nearly identical treatment occurs in *kharja* No. XXXIV, where a distressed young girl addresses her mother in the first line and again at the end of the third. There is a forceful repetition of *non* in *kharja* No. XIII, where a negative construction is used to affirm defiantly positive feelings, along with a fivefold repetition of the Romance vowel,

Non kero, non, un khillello illā al-samarello.[23]	I do not want any sweetheart, no, except for the dear brunet.

In No. XXV, the short trochaic repetition of the word, *diya* (day), almost sounds like the beating of a tambourine. It is a merry sing-song rhythm which fits the mood of a summer celebration. The *kharja* begins as follows:

¡Albo diya, eshte diya, Diya de al-^{c}Anṣara ḥaqqā![24]	Bright day, this day Truly is Saint John's day!

In contrast, a slow, mournful beat runs through *kharja* No. XXXVIII, and the repeated phrase, *de mibe*, falls at the end of the rhyming lines:

¿Ké fareyo o ké serad de mibe? ¡Habībī, Non te ṭolgash de mibe![25]	What shall I do or what will become of me? My darling, Don't leave me!

The masculine pronoun, *elle*, the equivalent of *él* (he), is also repeated as the object of parallel prepositions at the end of both verses of *kharja* No. XII:

Benid la pashqa, ay, aun shin elle, Laṣrando meu qurazūn por elle.[26]	The holiday is coming, ay, and I'm still without him. My heart is aching for him.

This use of the same word for rhyming in such a key position is not uncommon in either the Mozarabic verses nor in other schools of Romance poetry where parallelistic forms occur, such as the Galician, Portuguese, and Castillian. *Kharja* No. XVI also fits within the context of this tradition:

¡Ke tuelle me ma alma! ¡Ke kita me ma alma![27]	He is taking my soul! He is robbing my soul!

Like the solemn toll of a steeple bell, distress is given greater resonance and simplicity in this way. The *kharja* gives the impression of being an unstudied, spontaneous lament. If only the music had been preserved so that we could hear these poems sung today!

Critics and composers of classical Arabic verse normally scorn repetition, which involves no plays on words or variation. It is not surprising, therefore, that Ibn Sanā' al-Mulk included only one example of this in the *kharjas* of *Dār al-Ṭirāẓ*. It is found at the end of *muwashshaḥ* No. 34, composed by al-Tuṭīlī. Here the same words (*wāsh kān*) are used three times, and the reiterated personal pronoun, me (*nī*), recurs in the rhyming positions. In the transliterated version below, the arrangement of the parallel phrases can be seen clearly.

wāsh kān dahā-nī	How he has astounded me,
yā qawmu wāsh kān balā-nī	Oh, people! How he has afflicted me!
wāsh kān daᶜā-nī	How he has provoked me!
nabdal ḥabībī bi-thānī	I will barter my beloved for another.

The language of this *kharja* is colloquial and popular in tone.[28]

One type of lyric which the Arabic and bilingual collections have in common is the dawn song, which is found in the medieval repertoire of other countries also. Although only one such *kharja* is recorded by Ibn Sanā' al-Mulk, the dawn theme does appear in the main part of several Arabic *muwashshaḥs*, as has been demonstrated. In morning drinking songs, dawn is a merry time; but in the prevailing Arabic tradition, where lovers part after a night together, dawn brings sorrow, as in *kharja* No. 22.[29]

My beloved left at dawn and I did not say
farewell to him.
Oh, lonely heart of mine at night when I
remember!

According to Iberian literary convention, lovers meet at dawn, so daybreak is a time for rejoicing.[30] Mozarabic *kharjas* Nos. XVII and XIX conform to this tradition.

I will not sleep, Mother,
At the break of day
Abū al-Qāsim comes,
The face of dawn.

Kharja No. XIX is very similar to this:

Oh, my compassionate Mother,
At the break of day
Abū al-Ḥajjāj comes,
The face of dawn.

In both *kharjas*, the same phrase, *a rayyo de manyana*, is used for daybreak and the same metaphor is given for the beloved's bright face, *maṭrana*. We now know, thanks to the study of J. S. Révah, that *maṭrana* is another word in the

Judeo–Mozarabic dialect for dawn or morning.[31] This comparison of the beloved to a rising sun is often used in Arabic poetry, but that does not preclude the possibility of its being a universal image which would not have been borrowed from the Moors or directly translated by them into the Romance tongue. Is the *alba* in *kharja* No. VII dawn herself or is it a metaphor again?

> Come, oh, enchanter.
> A dawn with such dazzling splendor
> Calls for love when it comes.

The first line of *kharja* No. IV is equally ambiguous, for dawn may be the subject or the radiant face of the young woman's lover.[32] The image seems to have been popular, appearing in various Mozarabic *kharjas*. In contrast, the Arabic *kharjas* display a greater variety of themes and, if one can judge by Ibn Sanā' al-Mulk's anthology, they are not as repetitious.

So far, either the aspects which are unique to Mozarabic *kharjas* or which they share with Arabic ones have been considered. By no means should the elements contained in the *kharjas* of *Dār al-Ṭirāz*, which are missing in the Mozarabic texts, be overlooked. It may come as a surprise to those who are used to the exclusively amorous thematic content of the Mozarabic *kharjas* to find that the content of Arabic *kharjas* may also be panegyric or ascetic. Let us first look at several panegyric *kharjas*. Three of these emphasize uniqueness. Glory recites the following exclamation at the end of *muwashshaḥ* No. 19, written by Ibn Baqī, the only poet whose work is found in all three manuscripts being analyzed here:

> Truly Yaḥyā is the scion of noble lineage,
> Unique in the world, and the quintessence
> of mankind.

Ibn Baqī may also be the author of No. 17, which terminates with the poet reciting in the last *bait* and *kharja*:

> Say: "There is no substitute for him among those who dwell
> on earth." Say:
> "Don't you see that Aḥmad cannot be surpassed
> in his great glory?
> The West gave rise to him. So show us the
> likes of him, oh, East!"

The pride of being an Andalusian is reflected in this *kharja*'s open challenge. Aḥmad may have been just a *qādi* (judge), rather than an emir or caliph, but he seemed superior to anyone that the Eastern Arabic world had produced in the poet's eyes. Another composer of both Arabic and bilingual *kharjas*, Ibn ᶜUbāda, portrays woodland doves singing about the unparalleled merits of two famous Andalusian rulers of Almería and Seville in *kharja* No. 21:

Say, have there ever been known or experienced
  or have there been
Two rulers like al-Mᶜtaṣim and al-Muᶜtadid?

He has used a rhetorical question effectively to arouse wonder and admiration at the end of the *muwashshaḥ*. The listener answers it himself after the melody stops. The expected answer, "no," must have hung silently in the air for a moment.

Ibn al-Labbāna celebrates the ᶜAbbādid family of Seville, the one to which al-Muᶜtaḍid belonged, in *kharja* No. 12:

Banū ᶜAbbād, because of you we are enjoying festivals
And weddings. May you live forever for the people's
  sake!

In *kharja* No. 15, Ibn ᶜUbāda shifts his focus to Almería on the Mediterranean coast and emphasizes a similar state of festivity in the neighboring kingdom:

What a wonderful festival this is! The sand effuses
  a fragrance like amber for the one who walks
While the ships are like eagles, and al-Muᶜtaṣim is
  with his army on the shore.

Obviously, the merry atmosphere is attributed to al-Muᶜtaṣim's military strength and his ability to enforce peace in the area. Another military scene in Almería is depicted by Ibn ᶜUbāda at the close of *muwashshaḥ* No. 23:

When Ibn Maᶜn appeared with his clamorous army
And called each competitor by name in the challenge,
Then battle sang out while the sword rejoiced,
    "How beautiful is the army with its orderly ranks
    When the champions call out, 'Oh, Wāthiq, oh,
      handsome one!'"

Muḥammad al-Wāthiq may well be al-Muᶜtaṣim, both García Gómez and S. M. Stern believe.[33] In *kharja* No. 2, generosity is praised instead of military might. One of the Almoravid poets, probably Ibn Baqī or al-Tuṭīlī, both of whom wrote bilingual *kharjas* also, states:

I obtained what I desired when he was generous with
  gifts.
May God uphold the establishment of the magistrate
  of the city!

Apparently Abū al-Ḥusayn had handsomely rewarded the exiled poet who had previously been living in deprivation.

The *kharjas* of No. 5 and No. 32 deal with asceticism, as do verses in the main part of the poems, discussed in Chapter III. The fifth *kharja* is a taunt on the part of the poet's friends who want to tempt him to leave his newly found path of righteousness:

> Our companion has repented. Sing and serenade him!
> Present him with the drinking cup. Perhaps he
> will relapse.

In No. 32, al-Tuṭīlī regrets that he has abandoned the abstemious life of a hermit and fallen under the spell of worldly beauty:

> Love of beauties corrupted my asceticism and
> piety.

He presents this as a simple, straightforward fact that punctuates the end of his *muwashshaḥ*.

Certain images which are common to the main body of both Arabic and bilingual *muwashshaḥs* also appear in the *kharjas* of the Arabic collection. Bird imagery, which creates many diverse effects, often related to a lack of freedom or psychological captivity, brings the anonymous *muwashshaḥs* Nos. 6 and 8 to their close. The tone of the eighth *kharja* is melancholy. In the last *bait* we are told that a beautiful bird alighted for only a fleeting moment before taking wing again, leaving a sad lover behind to sing:

> If only you could have seen what kind of a bird
> alighted at my house and stopped beside me!
> When he saw the trap, he balanced his wings and
> departed with my heart.

The mood of the sixth *kharja* is different. "Sing about coquetry and send a message about humility," the poet exclaims in the line leading into the *kharja*. He has put up with enough:

> By God, oh, pampered bird brought up in the desert,
> Take care not to persist in your habit of throwing
> stones in my house!

The wind as messenger is another familiar Arabic motif which does not occur in the Mozarabic *kharjas* in either Ibn Bushrā's or Ibn al-Khaṭīb's collection, yet we encounter it at the end of *muwashshaḥs* No. 11 and No. 24 in *Dār al-Ṭirāz*. The poet who composed *kharja* No. 11 said, after his beloved left:

> Send the greeting with the wind for an anxious
> lover who does not trust mankind.

He believes that the wind is a more trustworthy messenger than other men he has known. The anonymous author of No. 24 describes with some perplexity one of his symptoms of lovesickness in the last *bait* and then addresses the breeze in the *kharja*, as follows:

> Oh, gentle breeze from my homeland, ask the loved
> ones how they are.

Gazelles do not appear in this corpus of bilingual *kharjas* either, whereas one is described as a finale to the hunting scene of *muwashshaḥ* No. 14 in the Arabic anthology:

> The gazelle crosses the plain and the greyhounds
> hasten behind.
> My sadness is nothing but guilty intentions which
> almost succeeded, but they did not overtake him.

The dramatic and swift narrative of the chase is interrupted by an introspective thought where feelings of guilt are briefly analyzed. The poet then returns to the chase to let us know that the gazelle slipped away without being captured. The parallel between the gazelle and the poet's beloved is obvious.

Why none of the bird, wind, or gazelle imagery appears in the Mozarabic *kharjas* is a question which cannot be answered with any certainty. Perhaps this involves a psychological difference between men and women, for metaphors like bird and gazelle, on the whole, are used by men in reference to their beloveds rather than vice versa. They tend to represent a masculine attitude, which seems to be the rule in the Arabic *kharjas*, but only the exception in the bilingual *kharjas*. Another possibility concerns the basic poetic traditions from which the *kharjas* may have been drawn. This imagery is commonly found in Arabic poetry, whereas it may not have been part of a previous Romance tradition. Because these *kharjas* are the oldest love lyrics in a Romance vernacular that we have at the present time, this conjecture cannot be documented by comparison with earlier texts, as can be done in the case of Arabic literature.

It is also typical of the Arabic *kharjas* to be more firmly woven into the thematic context of the preceding stanzas than their Mozarabic counterparts. In *Dār al-Ṭirāz*, the train of thought is rarely broken between the last *qufl* and *bait* before the *kharja*, which is definitely not so in the majority of bilingual texts. Transitions are less abrupt in the Arabic poems, and there is a more organic relationship of parts to the whole. In general, where the bilingual *muwashshaḥ* breaks off from the rest of the poem to insert a lyrical exclamation of joy or sorrow, a young girl's highly charged question addressed to her mother, or an imperative directed towards her lover, the Arabic *kharja* tends to continue the narrative thread of the last strophes right into the *kharja*. There is far less dramatic dialogue projected, and there are only a few deeply moving outcries in the Arabic series.

This tendency to flow more evenly from *qufl* to *bait* to *kharja* in the Arabic *muwashshaḥs* is visible not only thematically but structurally as well. In essence, this means that the Arabic *kharjas* are not treated as an artistic unity as often as the bilingual *kharjas* are. They are frequently bound more tightly to the total poem and are therefore more dependent upon it. In several of the Arabic *muwashshaḥs*, for example, there is no sharp syntactical division between the last *bait* and the *kharja*. This is the case in *muwashshaḥ* No. 25 by Ibn Zuhr:

> My heart is feverish and tears flow forth.
> He knows the sin yet will not acknowledge it.
> Oh, you who disclaim what I describe,
> My love for you has grown and increased. Don't say,
> where love's concerned, "I am a claimant!"

Here there is no true introductory verb, although "I describe" looks as if it were meant to perform that function. Nevertheless, it is enclosed within a clause modifying the beloved whom he is addressing. In No. 29, written perhaps by Ibn Baqī, the last line of the *bait* is similarly connected syntactically to the *kharja* through the use of an overlapping quotation. Al-Tuṭīlī's *muwashshaḥ* No. 32 does not shift speakers or have any syntactical break between the last *bait* and the *kharja*. It retains a narrative tone at the end:

> I have been an ascetic, or as I have been, but
> Love of beauties corrupted my asceticism and piety.

Parallel constructions are used in No. 17 to link the last two stanzas. The final line of the closing *bait* begins and ends with a form of internal dialogue turned outward to the audience. One exclamation follows the imperative, "say," in the *bait* and the second is situated in the *kharja*:

> Say: "There is no substitute for him among those who dwell
> on earth." Say:
> "Don't you see that Aḥmad can not be surpassed in
> his great glory?
> The West gave rise to him. So show us the likes
> of him, oh, East!"

This establishes a balance which detracts from the impact which the *kharja* is supposed to have.

In contrast, only one run-on *kharja* appears in the bilingual *muwashshaḥs*. It is No. XI, from Ibn Bushrā's text. In a departure from custom, the last line of the final *bait* is comprised of a totally Romance verse, whereas the ensuing *kharja* contains a mixture of the two languages:

Shi keresh komo bono mib	If you love me like a good man
Béjame idhā al-nazma dhūk,	Then kiss this string of pearls,
Bokēlla dhē habb al-mulūk.[34]	This little mouth of cherries.

A question might be raised about No. XXIIb, where the girl's conversation begins in the line above the *kharja*; but she herself introduces the *kharja* in Arabic. Although it is a complex construction, the presence of the introductory verb, to ask, along with the switch from Arabic in the last *bait* to the Mozarabic dialect in the *kharja*, sets the *kharja* apart as an independent statement. The same verses also appear as the *kharja* for *muwashshaḥ* No. XXIIa and have been separated from the rest of the poem in the usual manner.

Another stylistic device encountered in the Arabic *muwashshaḥs* is the insertion of a direct quotation in the second half of the *kharja*, as can be seen below in No. 23, by Ibn ᶜUbāda:

> How beautiful is the army with its orderly ranks
> When the champions call out, "Oh, Wāthiq, oh,
> handsome one!"

The use of one quotation within another is unusual, but it does not clash with the pattern described by Ibn Sanā' al-Mulk as long as there is a verb which introduces the *kharja*. According to him, this verb of introduction should be inserted just before the *kharja*. It looks as if the ruler of Seville, Muᶜtamid ibn ᶜAbbād, may have deviated from this commonly followed procedure in *muwashshaḥ* No. XXVI, because the introductory verb, to speak or say, is found at the beginning of his *kharja*. This is not certain, however, for the last *bait* is incomplete. It is interesting to notice that Muᶜtamid's *kharja* contains only two Romance words, *bokella* (mouth) and *esh* (this), in an Arabic framework. The language he is speaking is Arabic, with the substitution of two words from the Mozarabic dialect for two which he could have used in Arabic. There is not even one whole phrase of Romance in the *kharja*.

Kharja No. XXVI, in fact, is the only one from this bilingual group of *muwashshaḥs* which is written almost totally in Arabic. The majority of these Mozarabic *kharjas* are heavily weighted with Arabic words. In the Arabic collection put together by Ibn Sanā' al-Mulk, on the contrary, there are no Romance words, to my knowledge. Whether or not the Mozarabic in the bilingual *kharjas* corresponds exactly to the colloquial speech of al-Andalus's Romance-speaking populace at the time when the poems were written down, I do not know. This is a problem which lies outside the scope of this book. Nevertheless, it is worth glancing at the various types of linguistic interference which appear there with the hope of understanding the bilingual verses better. Many of the *kharjas* contain words which have simply been transferred from Arabic into the Mozarabic dialect. Given the social superiority of a conquering people over the indigenous population, it is not surprising to see this type of interference occur.[35] Where the Romance vocabulary was limited in a certain area (such as agriculture, to pick an obvious illustration), Arabic words filled in and became a permanent part of the language. In the case of some words used in the *kharjas*, however, we know that there were equivalents in Romance. For example, the beloved was called *ḥabīb* or *sīdī* instead of *amigo* or *señor*, and the Arabic style of address with *yā* before a noun was usually employed instead of a Romance form like *ay*. Presumably, social factors must be involved here. Given the fact that the girl being represented in these *kharjas* belongs to the conquered group of Mozarabs, it is only natural that she would address an Arabic-speaking man in his terms rather than hers, even though they are both bilingual. Because the poets and the men they praised were Muslims, not one of these *muwashshaḥs* depicts a young girl addressing a Mozarab man. Even if this had been so, the predominating social custom throughout the territory may have been to call one's sweetheart, *ḥabīb*, a fashion which could have penetrated the various strata of society.

In three *kharjas*, the type of parallelistic repetition which was noted earlier appears, but instead of using the same language, both Arabic and Romance are used.[36] *In* (Arabic) *non* and *si* (Romance) *non*, both meaning "if not," are set up as parallels in the fifth line of the first *kharja*; the negatives, *la* and *non* are used at the beginning and end of the same verse in No. XXII; and the phrase, "come to me," *jī* ᶜ*indī*, is repeated in Romance, *adúname*, in No. XXXV. This may have been done for the stylistic effect created by such bilingual parallelism, possibly as a virtuoso's play on the simple principle of unilingual repetition found in other *kharjas*, or it could have been an effort to bolster the comprehension of those listeners in Arabic-speaking circles who may not have been bilingual.

Another phenomenon which appears in the Mozarabic *kharjas* is the adaptation or integration of loanwords. At times, Arabic nouns and adjectives received Romance diminutive endings, *-ello* or *-ella*: *khil*(*l*)*ello* (friend) and *hamrella* (red). The Mozarabic dialect undoubtedly absorbed many words like these. Furthermore, as we saw in *kharja* No. XXVI, Romance words can be transferred into Arabic phrases. A good example of lexical transference operating in both directions can be seen in *kharja* No. XXXII:

¡Fēn ᶜindī, ḥabībī![37]	Come to me, beloved!
Shéyāsh sabiṭōre:	You must know
Ṭū huýda samāja.[38]	Your departure is loathsome.
¡Imshi, adūnū-nī!	Come on, join me!

Here ᶜ*indī*, *ḥabībī*, and *samāja* are intercalated in the Romance verses, and the process is reversed in the final Arabic line, where a Romance word is inserted.

Several Mozarabic *kharjas* use the syntax and vocabulary of both languages. Interspersed with Romance verses in some *kharjas* are very simple Arabic exclamations like *amānu*, *amānu*, *yā al-malīḥ* (Mercy, mercy, oh, handsome one) in No. V, a brief prepositional phrase such as *ka-al-wars* (like turmeric) in No. XX, or a nominal sentence like the one in No. XXII, *al-ghilāla rakhīṣa* (the tunic is fragile). These are a few of the less complex mixtures. As one might expect, there are varying degrees of complexity. *Kharjas* Nos. XXV and XXXVII both consist of four lines, three of which are in the

Mozarabic dialect, containing Arabic nouns, with a fourth line written completely in Arabic, whereas No. IX is composed mainly in Arabic with only the short Romance statement, *non t'amarey*, and one preposition, *kon* (*con*, with) in the first line. Others seem to be more balanced in their use of the two languages, incorporating verbs and complete phrases of both Arabic and the Mozarabic dialect, rather than just transferring nouns from one language to the other. *Kharjas* No. XXXI and No. XXXIV are good examples of this bilingual talent. Perhaps the most evenly balanced one is No. XXXII, quoted above. In the first line, the Romance verb, *fen* (*ven*, come) is combined with a prepositional phrase in Arabic *ᶜindī* (to me), followed by *ḥabībī*. Although the next line contains only Mozarabic words, the third and fourth lines contain a balanced mixture of Arabic and Romance, as the transcription clearly demonstrates. The bilingual balance of *kharja* No. XXVII by Ibn Baqī has led García Gómez to speculate that it was originally much shorter and that the poet may have added the third and fourth verses. Did Ibn Baqī, in fact, alter a popular *copla* which ends with the formulaic question, *¿ké farey*? as García Gómez assumes?[39] Or did he compose the whole *kharja*? The answer may never be proven, but the traditional nature of the formula at least provides a clue.

Only two bilingual *muwashshaḥs* contain *kharjas* that are written entirely in Romance. They are No. XVI and No. XVIII, taken from Ibn Bushrā's manuscript, and both are anonymous. One *kharja* is addressed to a young girl's mother, the other to her beloved. The two-line laments are straightforward and give the illusion of being quite unsophisticated. There is only minor variation in the parallelistic verses of No. XVI, where "many a young girl" cries out to her mother: "He is taking my soul! He is robbing my soul!"[40] A direct personal complaint is contained in No. XVIII: "Like someone else's child, you no longer sleep on my breast."

In addition to the problem of language, we are faced with the dilemma of rhyme schemes which present conflicting evidence about the origin of the *kharjas*. Before delving into specific examples, however, I would like to summarize as briefly as possible the salient differences between Romance and Arabic principles of rhyme which apply to the verses in question here. In Romance prosody, the vowel or dipthong in the last metrically stressed syllable of the line constitutes the basic vocalic rhyme element. Subsequent sounds may follow this, and in the case of paroxytons, the rhyme includes the entire unstressed syllable at the end. This produces pure Romance rhyme. If the vocalic elements of the rhyme are matched, but not the consonants, we have assonance instead. Homonyms are equally acceptable in both Romance and Arabic verse.

In Arabic poetry, on the other hand, position of the rhyming elements is more important than stress, which may vary in the spoken language from region to region. (Even a simple name like Aḥmad may be accented on the first syllable in the East and accented on the last syllable in the Maghrib.) The position of the syllables, of course, does not change. In general, Arabic meter is measured in terms of long and short syllables, although G. Weil has pointed out that stress also plays an important role.[41] According to Arabic tradition, the last syllable carries the rhyme. The main rhyming element is a letter called the *rawī*, which may be followed by either a long vowel or the letter, *h*, preceded by one of the short vowels. The final consonant and the vowel which accompanies it in the last syllable must remain constant throughout the rhyming sequence in Arabic. When compared to the final syllable, the penultimate syllable constitutes a more variable part of the rhyme pattern in Arabic. The last two syllables of *ḥabībī* rhyme with *qulūbī*, for example, and *yajmulū* is interchangeable with *taf*ᶜ*ilū*. In contrast to Romance versification, the metastasis of vowels is permissible in the penultimate syllable. In that position, the vowels, *i* and *u*, are interchangeable in Arabic. At times, a short *a* may be used in place of a short *i* or *u*, despite the fact that this is considered a fault. For instance, a word like *nusbalū* might be used to rhyme with the above examples, *yajmulū* and *taf*ᶜ*ilū*. According to W. Wright, "this fault is but a trifling one, and not seldom committed even by the best poets."[42] Only a long *a* in the penultimate syllable may never be altered. It is helpful to keep these canons in mind when trying to determine whether the bilingual *kharjas* conform to the norms of Arabic or Romance poetry.

When considering rhyme in the poems from *Dār al-Ṭirāz*, the question of possible Romance patterns does not arise, for all the *kharjas* were composed with Arabic rhyme schemes based on the last syllable. A few typical rhymes will illustrate this point: *-ān*, *-rī*, *-ān*, *-rī* in the *kharja* and other *qufls* of *muwashshaḥ* No. 1;[43] *-ād*, *-ād*, *-ās*, *-ās* in No. 12; *-āl*, *-lā*, *-tī*, *-āl*, *-lā*, *-tī* in No. 18; and *-lī*, *-lī*, *-lī* in No. 27. It should be added that both the Arabic and the bilingual *kharjas* may contain unrhymed lines interspersed with rhyming ones. This occurs in Nos. VII, XXVII, and XXX of the bilingual group and in Nos. 4, 6, and 33 among the Arabic *muwashshaḥs*, to cite just a few. Their respective rhyme schemes are ABB, AAABA, and ABCB in the former group and AAB, ABCDB, ABB in the latter. There are some *muwashshaḥs* which do not have any rhyming verses within the *kharja*'s single strophe, such as Nos. 3, 10, 24, and 25 in the Arabic anthology. The lines of their *kharjas* end in the following manner: *-rā*, *-īm* (or *-ūm*) in No. 3; *-nī*, *-*ᶜ*ū* in No. 10; and *-kā*, *-*ᶜ*ī* in No. 25. The bilingual *kharja*, No. XXXII, does not rhyme either, although in this instance, the same final vowel (Romance *e* or Arabic *i*) is repeated at the end of the words, *sabitore* and *adūnū-nī*.[44] This creates a homophonous sequence which binds the stanza together. Patterns like AB or ABCD are repeated in successive *qufls* which follow the *maṭla*ᶜ. This unifies the whole poem just as well as a rhyming pattern would. One can imagine that the music also added to this sense of unity, binding the strophes together with a recurring melody and rhythm.

Because the opening *maṭlaᶜ*,[45] when there is one, and the *qufls* of a *muwashshaḥ* are said to have been modeled on the *kharja*, a comparison of the thirty-eight bilingual *kharjas* with their corresponding *maṭlaᶜs* and *qufls* can give us further insight into the problem of the *kharjas*' cultural identity, even though it does not reveal conclusive evidence to support the theory that the *kharjas* were culled from preexisting Romance lyrics. The findings of this comparison merit detailed illustration, but first it will be useful to present them concisely. There are four *kharjas* out of thirty-eight in which Arabic words alone carry the rhyme (Nos. IX, X, XI, and XXV), and for this reason they cannot be used for drawing inferences about Romance verse patterns. Then, as mentioned above, *kharja* No. XXXII has no rhyme at all and must therefore be disqualified. The twentieth *kharja* must also be set aside because the rhyme word in the second line is still not clear enough for us to be certain that it is actually a Romance verb, and the word with which it rhymes at the end of the *kharja* is Arabic. This reduces the total involved here to thirty-two *kharjas*. In these *muwashshaḥs*, no unorthodox Arabic rhymes in the *qufls* have been caused by the parallelism with Mozarabic *kharjas*. The rhymes of twenty-three of these can be considered good from the point of view of both Romance and Arabic prosody (Nos. III, IV, V, VI, VII, VIII, XIII, XIV, XV, XVII, XVIII, XIX, XXI, XXII, XXIII, XXVI, XXVII, XXVIII, XXIX, XXX, XXXI, XXXIV, and XXXVI), as long as one allows for the fact that the Romance vowels, *e* and *o*, are equivalent to the Arabic *i* and *u*. Five *kharjas* contain rhymes which are acceptable by Arabic canons only (Nos. I, II, XXIV, XXXIII, and XXXV) and *kharja* No. XXXVII rhymes only if Romance assonance is taken into consideration. There are also three *kharjas* which contain Romance words that rhyme rather awkwardly with themselves (Nos. XII, XVI, and XXXVIII).

First, let us examine several of the Mozarabic *kharjas* whose rhymes meet the different requirements of both Arabic and Romance canons. Those whose rhyming words consist of Arabic nouns or adjectives with Romance suffixes fit into this category nicely. In No. XIII, the rhyme is based on the masculine Romance diminutive suffix, *-ello*, which conforms to the final *-lū* in the Arabic *qufls*; and in No. XIV, it is based on the feminine form of the same diminutive suffix, *-ella*, which becomes *-lā* in Arabic. In both cases, the bisyllabic Romance rhyme is shortened to a monosyllabic Arabic rhyme, based on the last syllable. Romance words which end in *-ore*, *-ire*, and *-are* are also found in this group, but they retain their bisyllabic nature in the Arabic *qufls*. The *kharjas* of No. IV and No. VII contain rhyming words which terminate with *-ore*, and they are matched by the final Arabic syllable, *-rī*, with a long *u* or *i* in the penult. (The Arabic-speaking poets measure the vowels in front of the *-re* in these words as a long vowel; if they were shortened in the *qufls*, it would interfere with the meter.) Similarly, in No. XV and No. XXXVI, where the Romance rhyme, *-ire*, occurs, the Arabic *qufls* adopt the *-rī*, preceded by a long *u* or *i*.

Only where Romance words ending with *-are* are concerned does the letter before the final Arabic rhyming syllable, *-rī*, remain constant. In accordance with classical Arabic rules, the vowel must always be a long *a*. *Muwashshaḥs* No. VIII and No. XXIX also have Romance words which are transliterated into Arabic with a long *a* before the final consonant. Their rhyme is based on nouns and verbs such as *amar*, *estar*, or *mar*, with the accented *-ar* in Romance becoming *-ār* in the Arabic *qufls*. The Romance rhyme words of No. XVIII, *alyeno* (*ajeno*) and *sheno* (*seno*), where the *e* is also measured as a long vowel, are matched in Arabic by *-īnū* (and *-ūnū*). Not all the rhymes in the bilingual *kharjas* consist of words from the same language. Some mix Arabic and Romance, producing such combinations as the following: *mībī* and *raqībī* in No. XXVIII, or *diya* and *nasī'a* in No. XXXIV. These rhymes conform to Romance norms in the *kharjas* but not necessarily in the *qufls*. In a poem like No. XXVIII, the long *i* alternates with a long *u* before the rhyme syllable, *-bī*, for example. This metastasis is typical in Arabic and, as used in the *qufls*, forms an acceptable parallel to the *kharja*'s pure Romance rhyme.

Among the *kharjas* which do not conform to the poetic canons of both Arabic and Romance, there is one which mixes the two languages in a similar way. No. XXXVII pairs the Arabic noun, *qaumu*, with *dad-lo* in Romance. This assonant Romance rhyme is not encountered with any regularity in the *qufls* of the *muwashshaḥ*. Only the final unstressed syllables, *-mū* and *-lū*, are used in the *qufls*, which is perfectly normal in Arabic. The Arabic verses thus form a pattern which does not rhyme at all. This lack of rhyme in a *kharja*, as discussed above, is permissible, although it does not occur with great frequency. Seen from the perspective of a critic schooled in Romance poetry, the *kharja* forms a quartet whose assonant rhyme scheme is ABCB. I think that this is the only *kharja* in which the rhyme meets solely Romance criteria.

Three of the *kharjas* contain Romance words which rhyme with themselves: *elle* in No. XII, *alma*[46] in No. XVI, and *mibe* in No. XXXVIII. Although this may not be technically incorrect, it is not considered good practice in either Arabic or Romance poetry. The Arabic *qufls* of these *muwashshaḥs* do not make the same mistake, it should be noted. They adapt the *-le*, *-ma*, and *-be* in their rhymes but do not use the same word twice in a couplet or tercet. The following rhyme words from a sample *qufl* in each of the *muwashshaḥs* concerned should serve to illustrate how this was done: *ṣillī*, *naṣlī* in No. XII; *dhammā*, *dhīmmā* in No. XVI; and *arībī*, *musībī* in No. XXXVIII. By any chance could the poets have been using these Romance words in order to match the Arabic pattern of their *qufls*? I would hope that these men were sufficiently bilingual and sophisticated to have used the same Romance word twice for a better reason than that, however. Perhaps the rules were being broken purposely in an effort to draw attention to the last lines. Just as the rules of classical Arabic could be broken in the *kharja*, it is conceivable that there was a parallel break with Romance rules of rhyme. Furthermore, if the *kharjas* were composed by people uneducated in the art of verse, or composed in an attempt to imitate an uneducated person's poetry, the repetition could also be seen in a different light.

There are five *kharjas* in which Romance words have been forced more obviously into post-tonic rhyme patterns that conform to Arabic standards alone. The rhymes found in Nos. I, II, XXIV, XXXIII, and XXXV are alien to Romance versification. In the first *kharja*, *nókhte* (*noche*) can rhyme with *férte* (*verte*) only if the last unaccented syllable, *-te*, is considered to be the rhyme element.[47] *Tánto* and *non tú* are combined in the second *kharja* in an equally disconcerting way. Only Arabic standards make sense here, where a final unaccented syllable, *-tu* (Romance *o* is written as *u* in Arabic script), and a stressed pronoun, *tu*, carry the rhyme. In Arabic prosody, this difference in stress, as pointed out above, is an unimportant matter. *Béjame* (*bésame*) and *huyóme* in No. XXXV also must have Arabic rules applied to them if any rhyme is to be found. The final unstressed *-me* (*-mī* in Arabic transliteration) is the only rhyme element in these two words, which make up the B-rhyme in the *kharja*'s pattern, AABAAB. The A-rhymes follow Arabic rules, too, repeating the final syllable, *-dī*: *ᶜiqdī*, *shuhdī*, *ᶜindī*, and *amandī*. *Kharja* No. XXXIII would also be acceptable to an ear attuned to Arabic verse, for all the rhyming elements are based on the last, unstressed syllables, *-rē*, *-mā*, *-rē*, *-mā*, which form the pattern, ABAB. *Amadóre* and *moríre* are paired at the end of the A-lines, where only a posttonic Arabic rhyme can be found. In the Arabic phrases, *fa mā* and *y'ummā* (a contracted form of *yā ummā*), there is a repetition of the final sounds, *a* and *mā*, which might be interpreted as a Romance rhyme. Nevertheless, the conjunction forming the penultimate syllable in the first B-line, *fa*, would not be as heavily stressed as the final, more important negative particle, *mā*, whereas the penultimate syllable in the vocative phrase, *y'ummā*, would receive the stress. It requires a stretch of the imagination to find Romance rhyme in these verses where Arabic canons have been followed so naturally.

By now it may be apparent that any Romance rhyme can be made to conform to Arabic rules by using the last consonant and vowel of each Romance line, even though it stands after the stressed penult, as the rhyme element. Pure Romance rhyme will produce an equally good rhyme in Arabic on the same basis. Assonant rhyme, where only vowels match, may result coincidentally, if Romance words are set in a nonrhyming Arabic pattern; for Arabic poetry needs a *rawī* accompanied by a vowel to tie the lines together. Because rhyme within the *kharjas* and *qufls* is not an absolute necessity, a repeating pattern is sufficient to bind the *muwashshaḥ* together. For this reason, any deviation from Romance canons in a Mozarabic *kharja* whose lines end with Romance words would indicate that it was not composed by a poet working within the framework of Romance prosody.[48] If the deviant rhyme conforms to Arabic standards, then that could point to the poet's being a bilingual Moor. He might also have been a Mozarab, living under Muslim rule and educated in the Arabic language, for race is not the issue. As we have seen, nine of the bilingual *kharjas* with Romance words in the rhyming positions fail to conform to the standards of good Romance prosody.[49] So it seems quite likely that at least some of the *kharjas* were composed expressly for the particular *muwashshaḥs* in which they are included. Moreover, not all of the Mozarabic *kharjas* sound as if they had been lifted from authentic Romance refrains. This does not mean, however, that *kharjas* which deviate from Romance norms may not have been taken from a preexisting source. There may have been popular songs composed in the Mozarabic dialect in accordance with the prosody of the region. We tend to forget that much of Arabic culture in al-Andalus was the culture of the Christian Mozarabs, too. Many of them spoke Arabic, adopted Arabic names and customs, and became so highly Arabized that it worried the Christian clergy. Even the Bible had to be translated into Arabic to be understood in some areas. Given this rich cultural admixture, it is not difficult to consider various possible sources for the Mozarabic *kharjas*. Some do resemble traditional Romance lyrics, while others fit into Arabic molds. For that matter, Ibn Sanā' al-Mulk did not specify a single tradition for the *kharjas* in his Arabic anthology either. Despite his lack of familiarity with Romance *kharjas*, he describes *kharjas* taken from colloquial Arabic, literary Arabic, and foreign sources, namely Andalusian. Possibilities abound, but concrete proof of each bilingual *kharja*'s origin is still lacking.

The meter of these poems presents another problem which has not been solved completely by any of the experts. Although quantitative meters are generally applied to classical Arabic poetry, because of the fixed duration of each syllable in the language, stress is also a factor which must be taken into consideration. García Gómez has already pointed out that the anapestic Romance meter coincides with three classical Arabic meters, *madīd*, *ramal*, and *munsariḥ*.[50] This comparison of Arabic meters to accentual Romance verse is particularly appropriate in connection with the *muwashshaḥ*, for it was considered a popular form of poetry. According to Gotthold Weil, stress not only prevails in popular Arabic poetry but "even gains in force when the songs are recited, because the stressed syllables are then emphasized by beating on instruments or by hand-clapping."[51] Perhaps the Middle Eastern specialists like Ibn Sanā' al-Mulk, who have had difficulty finding poems in classical Arabic that match the rhymes and metrical patterns of the *kharjas*, not to mention the whole *muwashshaḥ*, should have been looking for models among more popular genres. Spanish scholars, conversely, have had less trouble finding parallels. García Gómez, Menéndez Pidal, and Dámaso Alonso have located at least one authentic Spanish poem that is metrically similar to almost every *kharja* in both the Mozarabic and Arabic collections being discussed here.[52] In addition to Spanish *villancicos*, however, there may be some North African songs which match these poems. Certainly the *muwashshaḥ* is still being sung today in the Middle East and North Africa, but a detailed comparative study of this material still needs to be done. These lyrics, like the traditional Spanish verses to which the *kharjas* have been compared, would undoubtedly belong to a later period. Even so, the results of such a comparison would be interesting, in spite of the fact that they could not shed much light on the obscure origins and early development of the *muwashshaḥ*. Just as the existence of similar rhyme schemes and metrical patterns based on syllable count or patterns of stress cannot furnish concrete evidence that the *kharjas* were originally part of Romance poetry, neither would the existence of later poems in Arabic be able to prove that they originated in the Middle East or North Africa. Such facts do help in forming a workable hypothesis, and a study of this kind would be useful to Arabists and Hispanists alike. Although it might challenge the theories developed by Western scholars, it could also strengthen their arguments concerning the influence of Romance poetry on the *muwashshaḥ* and its *kharja*.

Meanwhile, the evidence we have indicates that the *muwashshaḥ* is a cultural hybrid, a type of poetry cross-fertilized in a multilingual, multicultural atmosphere.[53] Ibn Khaldūn, the famous fourteenth-century historian, expresses this process of literary cultivation in areas exposed to non-Arab influences very well:

> Now, poetry exists by nature among speakers of every language, since meters of a certain harmonious arrangement, with the alternation of (fixed) numbers of consonants, with and without vowels, exist in the nature of all human beings. Therefore, poetry is never abolished as the result of the disappearance of one particular language—in this case, that of the Mudar who, as everyone knows, were outstanding champions of poetry. In fact, every racial and dialect group among the Arab Bedouins who have undergone some non-Arab influence, or the urban population, attempts to cultivate poetry and to fit it into the pattern of their speech, as much as it suits them.[54]

The attempt to fit poetry into the new speech patterns and musical modes that develop in differing regions is not peculiar to the people of al-Andalus alone, although the *muwashshaḥ*, which seems to be one end result of this process, is undisputedly a unique creation of that area. After it was created there, its popularity spread to all parts of the Arabic-speaking world,[55] where it still gives joy to people, despite the fact that it was invented during Europe's Middle Ages.

Appendix
Historical Background: A Brief Sketch

Although the early history of the *muwashshaḥ* is still enigmatic, the identity of the man believed to be its inventor has been narrowed down to two quite similar names. In *Al-Dhakhīrah*, Ibn Bassām al-Shantarīnī (1070–1147) calls the inventor, Muḥammad ibn Ḥammūd (Maḥmud) al-Qabrī, the blind,[1] whereas the noted fourteenth-century historian, Ibn Khaldūn, gives his name as Muqaddam ibn Muᶜāfā al-Qabrī in *The Muqaddimah*,[2] slight variants of which are found in other manuscripts of the same work. These two names predominate in the literary and historical documents which refer to the invention of the *muwashshaḥ*, and scholars are still trying to determine which one is correct.[3] Although no one has recorded either man's birth or death, Muqaddam ibn Muᶜāfā al-Qabrī is listed among the poets under the emir, ᶜAbd Allāh ibn Muḥammad al-Marwānī (888–912),[4] which places him at the end of the ninth century and the beginning of the tenth. The original *muwashshaḥs* from this period have been lost, and no others appear on record for almost two hundred years. Due to this gap, we do not know to what extent the structure of the *muwashshaḥ* may have evolved during the first two centuries of its existence, whether it was born with a rigid form or whether it was slowly molded into the frame we have come to associate with this type of poetry. It has been assumed, however, that the form as we know it was created by its inventor in the late ninth century. Then in the latter part of the twelfth century, Ibn Sanā' al-Mulk made a formal analysis of the *muwashshaḥ* in *Dār al-Ṭirāz* (The House of Embroidery), a manuscript which has been lucky enough to survive the centuries. Thanks to this precise analysis, a concrete formula was provided for poets to follow.

To exemplify his descriptive theory, Ibn Sanā' al-Mulk included an anthology of thirty-four Andalusian *muwashshaḥs* along with an equal number of his own which follow the pattern of the ones from al-Andalus. Because he was an Egyptian, his own poems are of little direct interest for this study, but the Andalusian anthology is an invaluable source of comparison for anyone interested in the known corpus of Arabic *muwashshaḥs* with Romance elements in their *kharjas*. Not only are the *muwashshaḥs* which Ibn Sanā' al-Mulk composed peripheral to the study of Andalusian literary developments, but as poems they are considered to be fairly stiff and unnatural. According to Muṣṭafā al-Karīm, who wrote *Fann al-Tawshīḥ* (The Art of Writing *Muwashshaḥs*), this is typical of *muwashshaḥs* written in the Eastern Arabic world. It was a form with which Eastern Arabs were not completely at ease and, as a result, their attempts usually seemed affected when compared to the flowing rhythmic verses of al-Andalus.[5] This fact, al-Karīm believes, is the greatest proof of the *muwashshaḥ*'s Western origin,[6] a point which he does not need to emphasize, as eminent historians, Middle Easterners and Andalusians alike, have conceded that the *muwashshaḥ* is an Andalusian phenomenon.

Controversy which includes both European and Middle Eastern scholars has arisen over the basic influences involved in the creation of the *muwashshaḥ*. Some believe that it developed from an existing Arabic prototype, while others maintain that it must have been patterned after European models which were encountered in the Iberian peninsula and France. Those who feel that the *muwashshaḥ* grew out of the context of Arabic culture back up their point of view with examples of native poetic forms from which the *muwashshaḥ* could have evolved, and they strengthen their hypothesis with evidence of close cultural ties between the Eastern Arabic world and al-Andalus, demonstrating that such poetry could easily have been transmitted through this contact.

Although Arabic poems normally have only one rhyme throughout, a style had developed prior to the invention of the *muwashshaḥ* in which a verse could be broken up in several places, each one rhyming with the same part of the following verses:

____A ____B ____C ____D ____E ____F
____A ____B ____C ____D ____E ____F
____A ____B ____C ____D ____E ____F, etc.[7]

Some of these could be very complex and were often regarded as signs of decadence and cheapness by more traditional scholars and poets. Shorter lines were also employed. Although it is believed that these short, paired verses developed during the pre-Islamic period, the oldest examples are found in the tenth-century *Kitāb al-Aghānī* (Book of Songs). There we find, for example, a poem by al-Walīd ibn Yazīd, where the first verse rhymes with the second and the rhyme changes from pair to pair:

______________A ______________A
______________B ______________B
______________C ______________C
______________D ______________D, etc.[8]

The meter used in these short verses is apt to be a simple *rajaz*, which is usually a dimeter or trimeter whose basic foot is ⏑ — ⏑ —; or the meter might be a *ramal*, also a dimeter or trimeter, whose basic foot is ⏑ ⏑ — —. A. R. Nykl was well aware that Andalusian poets had access to these models, as he states that Muqaddam ibn Muᶜāfā al-Qabrī might have elaborated on the poems composed by the ᶜAbbāsid poet, Abū Nuwās (d. ca. 810), "without any necessity of seeking models in a *poesía andaluza romanceada*."[9]

The type which most closely resembles the *muwashshaḥ*, however, is the *musammaṭ*, whose exact age is not known, although it may possibly date back to the pre-Islamic period, as Imru' al-Qais is alleged to have used it.[10] Its stanzas may be put together in the following ways: AAB, CCB, DDB, etc.; AAAB, CCCB, DDDB, etc.; AAAAB, CCCCB, DDDDB, etc., and on to the most extreme eightfold arrangement. In each one, the B-rhyme must be repeated throughout. Originally, the rhyme had been incorporated into the last half of the hemistich. Later, an innovation occurred and the rhyme appeared at the end, as follows in the most common form, the *mukhammas*, which means fivefold:

______________A ______________A
______________A ______________A
______________B

When the five parts were written on one line, the B-rhyme came at the end, and the layout did not resemble the *muwashshaḥ*. The second form of the *mukhammas*, illustrated above, does resemble the *muwashshaḥ* so closely that they have often been confused. The *musammaṭ* and its fivefold version, the *mukhammas*, are written in classical meters, however, and do not conform to the stress-syllabic prosody found in *muwashshaḥs*. Another way of setting up the *musammaṭ* is to include a verse from another poet in the last two hemistichs, which is apparently its most famous form:

______________A ______________A
______________A ". . . . . .A
. . . ."B

Or it may be altered so that the quotation appears only in the last rhyming section:

______________A ______________A
______________A ______________A
". . . . ."B

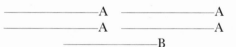

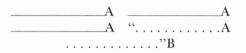

This variation is quite similar to the *muwashshaḥ*.

Ibraḥīm Anīs, Iḥsān ᶜAbbās, Martin Hartmann, and G. E. von Grunebaum have singled out this form as the possible, if not probable, ancestor of the *muwashshaḥ*. An excellent detailed study of a *musammaṭ* composed by Abū Nuwās was published by García Gómez.[11] Without giving up his belief in the influence of Romance lyrics on the *muwashshaḥ*, which he says is limited to the *kharja*, he discusses the possible fusion of the forms from both cultures. García Gómez is not alone, of course, in holding this down-to-earth compromise position.

Geographical distance did not prevent the Arabic-speaking world from remaining a cultural whole, even in times of political fragmentation. Cultural interchange was constantly maintained. Eastern scholars and manuscripts were brought by Andalusian rulers, such as al-Hakam II, to their courts and libraries, while travelers and pilgrims to Mecca often met the Eastern poets or learned their verses to recite to those at home. It is possible to single out certain men who were instrumental in this importation of Eastern *adab* (literary culture) to al-Andalus, such as Muḥammad ibn ᶜAbd Allāh al-Ghāzī or Hājir ᶜAbbās ibn Nāṣiḥ, who was particularly enthusiastic about the poetry of Abū Nuwās. Ibrāhīm ibn Sulaymān al-Shāmī encouraged the establishment of the postclassical school of poets in al-Andalus during the last days of al-Ḥakam ibn Hishām's reign (early ninth century), while Abū al-Yusr Ibrāhīm ibn Aḥmad al-Shaybānī, who had met such important members of this school as Abū Tammām, al-Buḥturī, and Diᶜbil (ninth-century poets also), studied their work and contributed to the dissemination of their poetry in the West. Other men went to Eastern centers of learning to study for a number of years, like ᶜAbd al-Mālik ibn Habīb (796-854), who studied Mālikite law in Madīna along with poetry of his favorite, Abū Tammām. On his return to al-Andalus he spread both legal teachings and poetry which he had learned in the Middle East.[12]

Iḥsān ᶜAbbās stresses the popularity of the "modern" or postclassical school in al-Andalus. Members of this group, like Abū Nuwās, Abū Tammām, and al-Mutanabbī, it should be noted, used the *musammaṭ*,[13] and they often used shorter forms or more complex and experimental styles. Abū Tammām, ᶜAbbās feels, was an important influence not only on form but on content in the Western Arabic world, awakening in the Andalusians an appreciation of nature which later came to characterize much of their poetry.[14] Other poets of importance were Ibn al-Rūmī (d. 896) and Ibn al-Muᶜtazz (d. 908), to whom the first *muwashshaḥ* had been mistakenly attributed by a number of scholars. The *muwashshaḥ* in question was probably composed by Abū Bakr ibn Zuhr al-Ḥafīd, although this has not been proven beyond all doubt either. At least it is not by Ibn al-Muᶜtazz, al-Bustānī has shown.[15]

In addition to books and scholars, the importation of singing girls, especially from Madīna and Mecca, continued during the reigns of the

Marwānids, ᶜUmayyads, and the fragmented *mulūk al-ṭawā'if* (petty kingdoms) later on,[16] not to mention the steady stream of Andalusian entertainers who were sent to the East in order to learn their arts at the source. Musicians also came from the East, the most famous of whom was a Persian tenor, Ziryāb, who had been at the court of Hārūn al-Rashīd until a jealous rivalry developed between him and his teacher, Isḥāq al-Mawṣilī, forcing the young singer to flee. He was invited to Cordova where he lived in lavish style under the patronage of ᶜAbd al-Raḥmān II (822–852). There he not only established new tastes in music and added a fifth string to the lute, but he set the style for fashions and manners as well. "He proved himself so polished, witty and entertaining that he soon became the most popular figure among the smart set of the time."[17] This popularity was at first limited to the ruler's palace, although it later spread from there to the general populace. While in Cordova, he founded a school of music. Other schools followed in Valencia, Seville, Granada, and Toledo. His sons carried on the tradition and their fame continued throughout the period of the small city states, finally spreading to the shores of North Africa.[18] Another influential figure in popularizing the Perso–Arabic system of music in al-Andalus was ᶜAbbās ibn Firnās, who died in 888. (Later, however, the Perso–Arabic system was replaced by classical Greek theories of music when they were translated into Arabic.)[19] Given this situation, there would naturally be Eastern critics like Fu'ād Rijā'ī, who believe that the innovating force of Ziryāb's methods was a strong factor in the creation of the *muwashshaḥ*.[20] ᶜAbbās also believes that the base from which the *muwashshaḥ* sprang may be found in Ziryāb's musical forms.[21] Regrettably, there is no written or recorded music from that period, so this is apt to remain a moot point indefinitely.

In terms of the close connection between music and the origin of the *muwashshaḥ*, they are not mistaken; for it is generally agreed by such scholars as Ibn Sanā' al-Mulk, al-Bustānī, and al-Karīm that the *muwashshaḥ* was composed in order to be sung. In this way, it differs from the *musammaṭ* and other Eastern verse forms which follow standard meters and can easily be recited, unaccompanied by music, without jarring the trained ear. Because of the unfamiliar stress-syllabic style of so many *muwashshaḥs*, it seems to be almost impossible for an ear well-trained in Arabic verse to appreciate them when they are recited rather than sung. Except in the few poems which are written according to classical meters, many Arabs claim that the *muwashshaḥ* must be set to music to be thoroughly enjoyed.

Concerning this problematical relationship between poetry and music, al-Jāḥiẓ (d. 869) makes a few pertinent remarks. The observation is made that the Arabs match their melodies to the meter of the poem. In foreign cultures, he comments, they may expand or contract their words and phrases in order to fit the tune. Strict forms of poetry are superimposed on a fluid, musical base.[22] Although he does not mention the *muwashshaḥ*, or any particular type of verse, for that matter, this generalized evidence is just one more clue in determining the origin of the *muwashshaḥ*, pointing perhaps to foreign influences.

García Gómez has attempted to clear up the mystery surrounding the meter of the *muwashshaḥ* for the Middle Eastern scholars and poets, not to mention for those of us in the West. He has asserted that syllabic count is the measure of many *muwashshaḥs* which could not be explained in terms of traditional Arabic meter. In a footnote to his study of *Dār al-Ṭirāz*, he comments about Ibn Sanā' al-Mulk's blindness regarding this point:

> ¡Que lecciőn se nos da aquí sobre la incomunicabilidad de las culturas y la dificultad de estos estudios comparativos! El autor, tan sensible a la prosodia árabe clásica—la prosodia de su raza—confiesa aquí cómo se le escapa el cómputo por sílabas, que a nosotros en cambio nos parece el único natural y el más fácil, y hasta afirma que sólo por la ejecución musical se aprecia la medida (!). Por lo demás, para nosotros, todas las muwaššaḥas tienen una cuenta silábica perfecta.[23]

Brian Dutton adds that it would have been natural for the *maṭla*ᶜ and *qufls*, which were patterned after Romance lyrics, to be forced into alien nonclassical metrical patterns in Arabic. Moreover, if Muqaddam ibn Muᶜāfā al-Qabrī was the inventor of this new form and if he came from an indigenous family that had recently converted to Islam, as his name suggests, then he would have grown up knowing the native Romance dialect and its unwritten poetic tradition.[24] Adapting Romance prosody to Arabic poetry would have been a creative challenge for a man with a bilingual background like that. When considering this possibility, James Monroe explains that the ᶜUmayyad dynasty was trying to create an atmosphere of racial harmony among the diversified population of al-Andalus at the time of the *muwashshaḥ*'s invention. This open attitude provided a favorable environment for the introduction and adaptation of non-Arab art forms.[25]

We do not know for certain that syllabic count was used in the Iberian peninsula around 900 A.D. when the *muwashshaḥ* was created, for no manuscript containing vernacular Romance poetry of that period has been found.[26] In the thirteenth century, *mester de clerecía* was introduced as something different and very learned, as can be seen at the beginning of *El libro de Alexandre* (ca. 1250):

> Mester trago fermoso, non es de ioglaria,
> Mester es sen peccado, ca es de clerezia,
> Fablar curso rimado per la quaderna uia
> A sillauas cuntadas, ca es grant maestria.[27]

Although syllables were counted in this form, it belongs to a learned clerical tradition which sets it apart from the Hispano-Arabic *muwashshaḥ*. Until examples of eighth-, ninth-, tenth-, and eleventh-century lyric poetry in old Spanish (any of the Hispanic dialects) are obtained, scholars must base their conclusions about the nature of the Mozarabic rhyme and meter on comparisons with lyrics from later centuries. Furthermore, Arabic meters based on patterns of long and short syllables could be treated in the same way. Since they generally repeat themselves, the same number of syllables would appear in each line. This might not be the case 100 percent of the time if the poet varied his verses. It is quite permissible to make the following substitutions, which would change the syllable count: ⏑ — ⏑ ⏑ — may become ⏑ — — —; ⏑ ⏑ — ⏑ — may become — — ⏑ —. Most variations, however, just alter the pattern of long and short syllables, as when ⏑ — — becomes ⏑ — ⏑, and ⏑ — — — becomes ⏑ — ⏑ — or ⏑ — — ⏑, to cite only a few instances. In addition, coincidences occur where meters of both languages can be measured in the same poem. García Gómez himself pointed this out:

> El anapéstico romance coincide, a la vez, con el *madīd*, con el *ramal*, y con el *munsariḥ*.[28]

The latter three are classical Arabic meters which correspond to anapestic Romance verses. It is possible, therefore, that the *muwashshaḥ*'s prosody was derived from models of Romance poetry.

Another factor which I feel should be briefly mentioned, despite the fact that a full discussion would exceed the compass of this study, is the litany of the Christian church. Its chants could be heard not only in al-Andalus, where Christianity was the religion of the conquered Visigoths, but in the Middle East where nuclei of Christians, mainly Copts, were to be found scattered here and there in towns and monasteries. The Christians were also a fine source of wine and might even be heard singing secular songs of their own outside of church grounds. In regard to popular songs of Spain and Provence, al-Karīm suggests that the church may have played a role in the development of secular styles.[29] Pierre Le Gentil is much more emphatic about this probability in his article on the *zajal*. Basing his study on the research of musicologists and liturgists, he sets forth a very convincing argument. The mesh of interrelationships is vast and this is just one more area to be considered in connection with the whole problem, as Pierre Le Gentil also admits.[30]

Some scholars restrict their theories of outside influences to European sources, in opposition to those who think that the *muwashshaḥ* emanated from Eastern models. They believe that the *muwashshaḥ* developed from songs of the jongleurs which the Arabs heard in Spain and France as the entertainers went from castles and homes of rulers to festivals and celebrations scattered through the land. Butrus al-Bustānī puts forth an argument for this side, explaining how the jongleurs' songs were free of constant rhyme and did not maintain the same form throughout.[31] In conjunction with this, Iḥsān ᶜAbbās states that between the second half of the ninth century and the beginning of the twelfth a number of Arabs in al-Andalus were influenced by neighboring styles in music. One was the singer, Husayn ibn ᶜAbd ibn Ziyād, who entered the northern territories, associated with the people there, and returned after a few years, having perfected their method.[32]

Such eminent Western scholars as García Gómez and Menéndez Pidal share this hypothesis which attributes a primary role to Romance poetry and song in the creation of the *muwashshaḥ*. Menéndez Pidal's well-known theory of the *estado latente* is expressed in an article on the *kharjas*:

> Sin duda; todos los países románicos tuvieron una lírica primitiva tradicional, derivada de espontáneos cantos latinos, consustanciales con la lengua latina vulgar, y con ella evolucionados hasta convertirse en cantos románicos.
>
> Esos cantos vivieron durante siglos en lo que hemos llamado *estado latente*, esto es, estado oculto de una actividad social cualquiera, cuya existencia no consta en ninguno de los testimonios coetáneos; actividad inadvertida por todos ellos, a causa de no merecer ninguna atención por juzgarla muy vulgar, insignificante, estraña a los usos corrientes aceptables.
>
> . . . El reciente descubrimiento de las muwaschahas con jarchya románica . . . nos deja prolongar la tradición de la canción andalusí hasta el siglo IX.[33]

García Gómez also subscribes to this theory, although he does not believe that every *kharja* is a faithful reproduction of this Romance technique and tradition. Leo Spitzer and Margit Frenk Alatorre add another dimension to this point of view when they discuss the similarities between many *kharjas*, Romance *chansons de femme*, and German *frauenlieder*. Spitzer believes that the *kharjas* prove Frings's hypothesis about a substratum of popular poetry preceding the troubadors.[34] Margit Frenk Alatorre, on the other hand, concludes one of her articles on this topic with another conjecture:

> No cabe hablar, probablemente, de una gran tradición lírica conjunta de la Romania (ni tampoco, a mi ver, de un tronco único dentro de España), sino de una serie de tradiciones distintas, de las cuales unas viajaron, mientras otras quedaron confinadas en una sola región. En cuanto al lugar de origen de esas tradiciones viajeras, difícil, si no ya imposible, será precisarlo.[35]

Romance poems and songs were not the only foreign ones to be heard in the Arabic-speaking world, however, nor was the *muwashshaḥ* the only innovation which developed in an atmosphere open to outside influences. During the first period of Islamic expansion, Persian slaves in Arabia played instruments and sang in accordance with their native styles. For example, Ṭuways (632–

710), the first musician to become famous under Islam, was brought up in al-Madīna in the household of Caliph ᶜUthmān's mother. The music of the Persians appealed to him, so he imitated it. He is believed to be the first to introduce the new music of his era, music which was heavily influenced by Persian styles.[36] Sā'ib Khāthir (d. 683) was another musician and singer from al-Madīna who learned the Persian modes, many of them from the popular Nashīt. When ᶜAbd Allāh ibn Jaᶜfar, his employer, marveled at Nashīt's skill and style, Sā'ib Khāthir said he could put Arabic poetry to the same kind of music. To the amazement of all, he proceeded to do this right away. Sā'ib Khāthir also originated a new rhythmical pattern (*thaqīl*) for Arabic songs which became quite popular.[37] In addition to Persian modifications, Byzantine ones were added by Ibn Muḥriz (d. ca. 715), a leper from Mecca who spent his life wandering from place to place. He is considered one of the four great singers of his time and, despite the fact that he did not appear at court himself, singing girls would introduce his songs there for him.[38] He traveled to Persia to gather material and then to Syria and the northern regions. By adapting what he liked from the Persian and Byzantine (*rūmī*) styles and discarding what did not appeal to him, Ibn Muḥriz produced a kind of music which had not been heard before, a hybrid. He is also credited with introducing the *ramal*, a new rhythmic mode, and with being the first man to sing in couplets (*zauj*), an innovation which allowed individuals to continue singing indefinitely without ending the melodies.[39] The mulatto, Maᶜbad (d. 743), also mixed Persian, Byzantine, and Arabic modes, coming up with new melodies in a grandiose style.[40] This made him the foremost singer of his time and a favorite of the caliph, Yazīd II.[41] On the whole, the traditional Arabic *qaṣīdas* were not affected by these musical changes, but one can see that, along with the old meters and forms, innovations that deviated from standard patterns of the past were appearing in the Middle East.

It is not difficult to imagine the same type of developments taking place in al-Andalus, as well as the inevitable importations of new Eastern modes into the Western spheres of the Muslim empire. Exactly what kinds of song existed in the Iberian peninsula at that time, we do not know. They were probably as new to the classical Arabic style as the Persian ones were, if not more so. Nevertheless, no one is certain that this is the case. Gustave von Grunebaum has already flung open the door of speculation regarding this point in a brief article on Romance lyrics before the Arabic conquest:

> It may, however, be useful to insist that the character *sui generis* which the "Spanish" songs of the first century A.D. doubtless possessed is likely to have been moulded under the impact of "Oriental" influences. . . . Equally if not more important is the fact—not hitherto considered as far as this writer is aware—that "Oriental" and in this particular case presumably North African influences on a "Romance"

> speaking Spanish-Christian audience can, at least in one specific instance, be traced a few decades before the end of the Visigoth rule.[42]

Von Grunebaum then cites the autobiography of Saint Valerius (ca. 630–695), who was born a Visigoth noble in Asturias, and relates his comments about a barbarous black Ethiopian who had been ordained as a second presbyter in Valerius's new church. Valerius attributes this ordination to the popularity among his patrons of Iustus's love songs, a very bad influence indeed, not to mention the other savage incantations which ended with the singer in an unconscious state after dancing himself to the point of exhaustion. Regarding this, von Grunebaum goes on to say:

> The combination of erotic minstrely with survivals of an orgiastic cult as late as the last third of the seventh century deserves notice. It is probably correct to label the songs of Iustus (who may not have been as singular a figure as he appears from the scarcity of our sources and the bias of St Valerius) the earliest concrete evidence of "Oriental" poetry and singing in Spain; the very success with which the priestly *joculator* met testifies to the strong appeal of this alien artistic strain; more important still, his success would be difficult to understand unless one assumes that he used the local *patois* or a language closely akin to it. The conclusion is hardly avoidable (that) the "Romance" in or resembling what the Arabs were later to describe as the *tarīqat al-Naṣāra* antedates the arrival of the Arabs on the Peninsula by some time. For there is nothing in the narrative of the injured saint which would suggest that Iustus was the first *joculator* of this kind.[43]

This possibility has not been given enough consideration. The intermingling of people from different cultures and the artistic skills they carry with them is not a phenomenon which begins in a particular year after some historic battle. It is a constant process, affecting civilizations during both periods of peace and war, given the natural mobility of man and his innate curiosity to know and explore other areas beyond his own town or country. Therefore, I do not believe that distinct lines or spheres of influence can be drawn at any one time. There is a constant flux and interplay among diverse cultures which we may never be able to disentangle to our satisfaction. This should be kept in mind when dealing with such singular creations as the *muwashshaḥ*, which should be viewed in its cultural context as a whole rather than as an isolated thing to be examined only in the pages of a manuscript or book.

Despite the fact that music may seem somewhat peripheral, it should be remembered that the *muwashshah*, in contrast to the traditional *qaṣīdas* or even the *musammaṭ*, was composed from the very beginning to be sung. The predominating attitudes towards song and musical theory are therefore of interest, because they indicate aspects of the cultural climate in which the *muwashshaḥ* was born. With the accession of the ᶜAbbāsid dynasty in 750, non-Arabic influences increased and valuable contributions were made by the translation of ancient Greek theories of music. The Perso-Arabic school was overwhelmed by those who followed the Greeks. Rather than get into a technical musical discussion, for which I am not qualified, however, I will just give a few examples of the Greek works which entered Middle Eastern culture during this period. According to a respected tenth-century survey of culture, *The Fihrist of al-Nadīm*, Nicomachus's major work on music was translated, along with Aristoxenus's books on harmony and rhythm.[44] Two attributed to Euclid are the *Kitāb al-Nagham* (Book of Notes) and *Kitāb al-Qānūn* (Book of the Canon).[45] From translations of Aristotle's *De Anima* and *Historia Animalium*, along with Galen's *De Voce*, Arabic scholars gleaned a lot about the physiological and physical aspects of the theory of sound.[46] These books elevated the study of musical theory to the point where it became one of the courses of scientific study in a student's curriculum. An atmosphere of tolerance tended to prevail in the courts, so it became acceptable to leave the traditional Arabian schools and experiment with new forms. Consequently, the repertoire of Arabic music grew and was enriched by this process.[47] One can easily see that this was a period of eclectic interests when the Arabs were constantly absorbing aspects of the diverse cultures with which they came in contact.

Not everything was readily accepted, though. A prime example is the *muwashshaḥ*, which was rejected as fine art at first in high learned circles of the Arabic-speaking world. It was categorized there as popular art, not as poetry.[48] The fact that it was scorned by traditionally minded Arabic poets and left out of literary collections of the time is a strong suggestion of its humble popular, if not foreign, origin. Singers took great delight in the new form, and its popularity grew to the point where it was finally accepted in all strata of society. Nevertheless, Eastern Arabs never succeeded in composing natural-sounding *muwashshaḥs*. According to Ibn Khaldūn, "the attempts at *muwashshaḥs* by Easterners are obviously forced."[49] The only exception he mentions is a *muwashshaḥ* composed by Ibn Sanā' al-Mulk. Given the Eastern Arabs' high level of sophistication and ornate, elegant styles, their awkward handling of the *muwashshaḥ* indicates that it was a Western creation and not just another Eastern *musammaṭ* put to music, as several scholars have maintained. Yet the existence of such strophic forms in the Middle East may have set the stage for the appearance of other types, not too distantly related, in al-Andalus.

Andalusian Poets Included in the Collections of Ibn Bushrā, Ibn al-Khaṭīb, and Ibn Sanā' al-Mulk

Name	Date century A.D.	Poem Nos.
Ibn al-Muᶜallim, Abū al-Walīd Muḥammad ibn ᶜAbd al-ᶜAzīz	mid-eleventh	VIIa
Ibn Arfaᶜ Ra'suh, Abū Bakr Muḥammad	mid-eleventh	XXXa, XXXI
Ibn Labbūn, Abū ᶜĪsā	mid- to late-eleventh	XXXVII and possibly XXIb*
Al-Muᶜtamid ibn ᶜAbbād, Abū al-Qāsim Muḥammad	d. 1095	XXVI
Al-Jazzār, Abū Bakr Yaḥyā al-Saraqusṭī or al-Baṭalayausī	late eleventh	XXVIIIb
Ibn ᶜUbāda al-Qazzāz, Abū ᶜAbd Allāh Muḥammad	late eleventh	9, 15, 21, 23, I, XX, and probably 18, VI
Al-Kumait al-Gharbī, Abū Bakr ᶜAbd Allāh Muḥammad ibn al-Hasan	late eleventh and possibly early twelfth	XIII, XXXII, and probably XV
Ibn al-Labbāna, Abū Bakr Muḥammad ibn ᶜĪsā al-Dānī	d. 1113	11, 12, XXIX, and probably 8, 13

Al-A^{c}mā al-Tuṭīlī, Abū al-^{c}Abbās Aḥmad ibn ^{c}Abd Allāh ibn Hurayra al-^{c}Absī	d. 1126	1, 30, 32, 34, II, V, VIII, XIX, XXV, and possibly 2, 5,† 14,† 22,† 28,† 31
Ibn Baqī, Abū Bakr Yaḥyā ibn Muḥammad ibn ^{c}Abd al-Raḥmān al-Qaisī al-Qurṭubī	d. ca. 1150	19, 20, 26, 27, 33, XII, XXIIa, XXVII, XXVIIIa, and possibly 5,† 10, 14,† 17, 22,† 28,† 29
Al-Manīshī, Abū al-Qāsim	mid-twelfth	XXXIV
Ibn Ruḥaym, Abū Bakr Muḥammad ibn Aḥmad	mid-twelfth	XXIIb, XXXVIII
Al-Aṣbāḥī al-Lāridī, ^{c}Abd Allāh ibn Hārūn	d. 1155	XVII
Al-Khabbāz al-Mursī, Abū al-Walīd Yūnus ibn ^{c}Īsā	probably mid-twelfth	XXIa, XXXVI
Ibn al-Ṣayrafī, Abū Bakr Yaḥyā	d. 1174	XXXV
Ibn Mālik al-Saraqusṭi, Abū Bakr Aḥmad	probably mid-twelfth	XXXb
Ibn Zuhr, Abū Bakr Muḥammad ibn Abī Marwān ^{c}Abd al-Mālik ibn Abī ^{c}Alā'	d. 1198	25
Ḥātim ibn Sa^{c}īd	probably late twelfth and early thirteenth	3
Ibn Luyūn, Abū ^{c}Uthmān	d. 1349	XXIb†

* Scholars do not agree about the author of this poem. E. Lévi-Provençal and García Gómez think that Ibn Luyūn composed it, whereas Stern and Solá-Solé believe that it is by Ibn Labbūn. See Stern, "Four Famous Muwaššaḥs from Ibn Bušrà's Anthology," *Al-Andalus*, XXIII (1958), p. 340, n. 1, and García Gómez, *Las jarchas romances*, p. 405, along with Solá-Solé, op. cit., p. 97, n. 1.

† Poems which may have been written by either Al-A^{c}mā al-Tuṭīlī or Ibn Baqī.

GLOSSARY OF ARABIC TERMS

Al-Andalus	The area of Spain ruled by the Muslims during the Middle Ages, which includes all but the northernmost regions of the Iberian peninsula.
bait	The part of a *muwashshaḥ* which repeats its meter and number of parts, but not its rhyme, and alternates with the *qufl* throughout the poem.
ghazal	Love poem
ḥabīb	Beloved, sweetheart
ḥājib	Chamberlain
imām	Prayer leader
Kaaba	The building in Mecca which houses the sacred Black Stone, towards which Muslims throughout the world turn to pray. It is also the most important point in the Islamic pilgrimage.
kharja	Literally, "exit." It is the last *qufl* of the *muwashshaḥ* and generally consists of colloquial or non-Arabic verses.
Maghrib	The Western part of the Arab world, including North Africa and al-Andalus.
maṭla^{c}	Opening verses which comprise the *muwashshaḥ*'s first *qufl*.
Mozarabic	The Romance dialect which evolved from Vulgar Latin, primarily spoken by Christians and Jews in Muslim Spain. This term was derived from *musta*^{c}*rib* (See below).
mulūk al-ṭawā'if	Small kingdoms into which al-Andalus was divided after the collapse of the ^{c}Umayyad dynasty (1031) and continuing until the region was conquered by the North African Almoravid dynasty (1091).
mukhammas	A *musammaṭ* whose stanzas consists of five parts, with the

	following rhyme scheme: AAAAB, CCCCB, etc.
musammaṭ	A strophic poem, written in classical Arabic, in which the last line of each stanza repeats the same rhyme. A typical rhyme scheme would be AAAB, CCCB, DDDB, etc., although each stanza may contain as many as eight parts.
mustaᶜrib	Someone who has adopted Arabic customs.
muwashshaḥ	Strophic poem, divided into *baits* and *qufls*, which developed in Muslim Spain during the Middle Ages. A typical rhyme scheme is XYZ, AAAAXYZ, BBBBXYZ, CCCCXYZ, DDDDXYZ, and EEEEXYZ.
qāḍī	Judge
qaṣīda	Classical Arabic ode which consists of conventional motifs and dates back to the pre-Islamic period in Arabia. It maintains the same rhyme and meter throughout and usually includes an erotic prelude, heroic episode, and panegyric.
qufl	The part of a *muwashshaḥ* which must repeat itself in meter, rhyme, and number of parts, alternating with the *bait* throughout the poem.
raqīb	Spy or guardian
rawī	The letter which forms the essential part of an Arabic rhyme scheme, repeating itself at the end of each verse.
sunna	Deeds and sayings of the Prophet Muḥammad.
waqf	Religious endowment or foundation.
washshāḥūn	Poets who compose *muwashshaḥs*.
zajal	Strophic poem resembling the *muwashshaḥ*, but composed in colloquial rather than classical Arabic. Only one line of the opening verses is repeated at the end of each strophe. A typical rhyme scheme is AB, CCCB, DDDB, EEEB, etc.

Notes

INTRODUCTION

1. S. M. Stern, *Les Chansons Mozarabes* (Palermo, 1953); reprinted Oxford, 1964. Stern's original article on this subject, "Les vers finaux en espagnol dans les muwaššaḥs hispano–hebraïques: une contribution à l'histoire du muwaššaḥ et à l'étude du vieux dialecte espagnol 'mozarabe'," appeared in *Al-Andalus*, XIII, in 1948. It has been translated and published in his posthumous volume, *Hispano–Arabic Strophic Poetry*, ed. by L. P. Harvey (Oxford, 1974), pp. 123–60.
2. Emilio García Gómez, *Las jarchas romances de la serie árabe en su marco* (Madrid, 1965).
3. Jawdat Rikābī used two manuscripts for his edition: No. 2038 from Dār al-Kutub in Cairo, which is the earliest copy dating to the thirteenth or fourteenth century at the latest, and manuscript No. 2047 in Leiden, which is a later and more complete version copied during the seventeenth century. For further information see Jawdat Rikābī, ed., *Dār al-Ṭirāz*, by Ibn Sanā' al-Mulk (Damascus, 1949), pp. 16–20.
4. Although I have not had access to the manuscripts containing the bilingual *muwashshaḥs*, I have been able to use the transliterations published by Emilio García Gómez in *Las jarchas romances en la serie árabe en su marco*, based on the text of Ibn Bushrā in the library of G. S. Colin and on *Jaish al-Tawshīḥ* by Ibn al-Khaṭīb. Concerning Ibn Bushrā's manuscript, see García Gómez's article, "Veinticuatro Jarŷas romances en muwaššaḥs árabes," *Al-Andalus* XVII (1952), pp. 63–64. Comments about Ibn al-Khaṭīb's collection are found in *Las jarchas romances*, p. 256. In this book, I have limited my study to the bilingual *muwashshaḥs* found in these two texts. The most complete collection of *kharjas* containing Romance words are found in Solá-Solé's *Corpus de poesía mozárabe* (Barcelona, 1973). James Monroe has published two additional examples in his article, "Two New Bilingual *Ḫarǧas* (Arabic and Romance) in Arabic *Muwaššaḥs*," *Hispanic Review*, XLII (1974). In total, there are sixty-two Mozarabic *kharjas* which have been found in both Arabic and Hebrew *muwashshaḥs*.
5. The question of Ibn ᶜUbāda's identity is discussed by S. M. Stern in *Al-Andalus*, XV (1950), pp. 79–109.
6. The primary differences between the *zajal* and the *muwashshaḥ* are in the former's use of colloquial rather than classical Arabic and in the repeating pattern which is woven into each stanza throughout the poem. The second element of every strophe in a *muwashshaḥ* is an exact metrical duplicate of the entire opening *maṭlaᶜ*, when there is one, or of the entire closing *kharja*, whereas in the *zajal* the end of every strophe matches only one line of the opening *maṭlaᶜ*. Moreover, a *zajal* does not have a *kharja* at the end, although there are exceptions to this rule: Ibn Quzmān did

compose some *zajals* that look like *muwashshaḥs* in the vernacular. Then to judge from what can be gathered from such Muslim scholars as Ibn Saᶜīd or Ibn Khaldūn, the acceptance of the *zajal* as a literary form followed the entry of the *muwashshaḥ* into the mainstream of Arabic literature. Whether it existed concomitantly with the *muwashshaḥ*, we do not know. García Gómez has indicated that the proliferation and popularity of the *muwashshaḥ* during the twelfth century may have been an attempt on the part of the poets to reach a more diversified audience after the Almoravid invasion. Unlike the *mulūk al-ṭawā'if* whom they replaced, the North African Almoravids did not appreciate the subtleties of classical Arabic poetry, so the poets suffered accordingly. Further information about their plight is given in García Gómez's *Un eclipse de la poesía en Sevilla: la época almorávide* (Madrid, 1945). The *zajal*, then, may have been a necessary transformation of the *muwashshaḥ* in which the poets used colloquial expressions and more popular imagery in order to reach more people and thereby survive. For more details about the *zajal*, see S. M. Stern, "Studies on Ibn Quzmān," *Al-Andalus*, XVI, 1951, pp. 379–425, which has been reprinted in *Hispano-Arabic Strophic Poetry*, pp. 166–203, and García Gómez, *Todo Ben Quzmān*, 3 vols. (Madrid, 1972).

CHAPTER ONE

Ibn Sanā' al-Mulk's Theory of the *Muwashshaḥ*

1. The first written record of the *muwashshaḥ* is found in *Al-Dhakhīra* by Ibn Bassām al-Shantarīnī (1070–1147), who seems to have relied on the work of an earlier author, ᶜUbāda Ibn Mā' al-Samā', who died around 1030. For more detailed information about early sources, see S. M. Stern, *Hispano–Arabic Strophic Poetry*, pp. 3–11, 63–80. The earliest extant collections containing Arabic *muwashshaḥs* with Mozarabic *kharjas* were compiled by Ibn Bushrā and Ibn al-Khaṭīb, who lived during the fourteenth century. All are quite far removed from the late ninth or early tenth century, when the *muwashshaḥ* first appeared. Earlier texts may turn up in the future, but for now we must be content with what is at hand.

2. Ibn Khaldūn (1332–1406) states that a *muwashshaḥ* "consists of 'branches' (*guṣn*) and 'strings' (*simṭ*) in great number and different meters." He does not even mention the final *kharja* in his short description of this poetic form, found in *The Muqaddimah*, trans. by Franz Rosenthal, vol. 3 (New York, 1958), p. 440. Ibn Bassām (1070–1147), on the other hand, says that the *muwashshaḥ* was made of hemistichs (*shaṭr*) of classical poetry, using mainly neglected and unused meters, and a *markaz* at the end which contained colloquial and foreign words or phrases. *Markaz* is the term he uses for *kharja* in *Al-Dhakhīrah fī Maḥāsin Ahl al-Jazīrah*, ed. by Ṭāhā Ḥusayn, vol. 1 (Cairo, 1946), pp. 1–2.

3. E. García Gómez, "Estudio del *Dār aṭ-Ṭirāz*," *Al-Andalus*, XXVII (1962), pp. 28–104.

4. For striking parallels between the Arabic words used to describe the parts of a *muwashshaḥ* and certain Romance terms from which they could have been derived, see Brian Dutton, "Some New Evidence for the Romance Origins of the *Muwashshaḥs*," *Bulletin of Hispanic Studies*, XLII (1965), pp. 73–81 and James T. Monroe, "Hispano-Arabic Poetry during the Caliphate of Cordoba: Theory and Practice," in *Arabic Poetry*, ed. by G. E. von Grunebaum (Wiesbaden, 1973), pp. 133–134, n. 26.

5. It is not at all uncommon for poets to use *kharjas* found in earlier poems. For example, the twelfth-century poet, Ibn Baqī, chose a line written by Ibn al-Muᶜtazz (861–908) for the *kharja* of one of his *muwashshaḥs* (No. 26). At a later date, the fourteenth-century poet, Abū ᶜUthmān ibn Luyūn used the same *kharja* employed by another Andalusian, al-Khabbāz al-Mursī, in Nos. XXIa and XXIb. If a mistake has been made in the manuscript and Ibn Labbūn (XIth century) actually composed XXIb, as Stern and Solá-Solé assume, then al-Khabbāz al-Mursī (probably mid-XIIth century) must have borrowed the *kharja* from Ibn Labbūn or perhaps some other source.

6. García Gómez, "Estudio del *Dār aṭ-Ṭirāz*," loc. cit., pp. 55 and 59.
7. The few *muwashshaḥs* in which both *bait* and *qufl* have the same meter reminded him of the *mukhammas*, an atypical fivefold strophic poem which is composed in accordance with classical metrics.
8. García Gómez, "Estudio del *Dār aṭ-Ṭirāz*," loc., cit., p. 48.
9. García Gómez, "La 'Ley de Mussafia' se aplica a la poesía estrófica arabigoandaluza," *Al-Andalus*, XXVII (1962), pp. 1–20.

CHAPTER TWO

Translation: An Andalusian Anthology in *The House of Embroidery*

1. Literally, "He lifted me up and put me down."
2. This verse contains a typical play on words. Both nouns stem from the same triliteral root, *ᶜain, dhāl, rā'*.
3. *Laisa*, in the original text, was corrected by García Gómez to *aysh*, the colloquial phrase, "what is wrong," in "Estudio," loc. cit., p. 66.
4. The rising and setting sun.
5. Travels here refer to dreams in which the beloved would appear.
6. A literal translation would be: "Who could cover (or come to) his pillow?"
7. Fountain or spring and eye are the same word in Arabic.
8. Literally, "saliva."
9. Literally, "His age is watered by the one who is as generous as the moisture of meadows from clouds."
10. Literally, "It lent the gazelle glances and a slender neck."
11. In other words, it is perfect.
12. This is an idiom which means "to walk proudly," but because of its vivid imagery, I chose to translate it literally.
13. The literal rendition of this is: "Beauty established armies on his pupils."
14. In Islam, magic is usually prohibited, although there can be legitimate charms such as phrases from the Koran.
15. García Gómez defines *qūqū* as *golosina* (sweet morsel, bonbon) in "Estudio," loc. cit., p. 74. It might also be just a nonsense word.
16. This is a way of indicating that what was unsheathed can't be described.
17. The Banū ᶜAbbād made him wealthy (provided his wings with feathers) and then he became obligated to them, as indicated by the symbolic ring which they put around his neck.
18. Yaᶜrub is a mythical king of Yemen and ancestor of the Ḥimyarite kings. The Berbers claimed that they descended from the Ḥimyarites.
19. This refers to the bubbles which form when water and wine are mixed.
20. The sea is a metaphor for great and generous men.
21. Hārūn al-Rashīd, the famous ᶜAbbāsid caliph of Baghdad.
22. The *ᶜuwwād* are visitors who call on sick people.
23. Literally, the *thumād* are puddles drying up in summer.
24. Salsabīl is the name of a spring in Paradise.
25. The river Kauthar in Paradise.
26. Literally, the day of al-Baqīᶜ, a pre-Islamic day of battle.
27. Al-Amīn, who repudiated his father's will and tried to take the throne away from his brother, Hārūn al-Rashīd.
28. The smile of the beloved is compared to a flash of lightning.
29. A proverbial wise man.
30. Literally, "since he parted or since I parted."

31. Wine in Arabic is spelled with the letters *khā'*, *mīm*, and *rā'*, and cheek begins with *khā'*, smile with *mīm*, saliva with *rā'*.
32. More literally, "Some parts of me cried over parts of me with me."
33. The imagery here is feudal. The poet has assumed an obligation to cultivate love as a tenant farmer cultivates land, and in return he expects security.
34. "Darkness of the night" is a metaphor for black hair in this case.
35. See S. M. Stern, "Four Famous Muwaššaḥs, from Ibn Bushrā's Anthology," *Al-Andalus*, XXIII (1958), p. 355, and García Gómez, "Estudio," loc. cit., p. 94.
36. These images, which pertain to fine horses, convey the idea that his attributes are unsurpassed.
37. *Sunna* means the deeds and sayings of the Prophet Muḥammad.
38. The Arabic verbs in this sentence represent the colloquial Andalusian/Maghribī form of the first person singular. See Stern, *Hispano–Arabic Strophic Poetry*, pp. 39–40.
39. Another reading for *rummān* (pomegranate) is zamān (time). See García Gómez, "Estudio," loc. cit., p. 100.
40. See above, note 37.
41. Literally, "His soul is between the collarbones."

CHAPTER THREE

Commentary on Ibn Sanā' al-Mulk's Andalusian Anthology

1. For the Arabic text of Ibn Zuhr's poem, see Ibn Khaldūn, *Tarīkh al-ᶜAllāma*, 2d ed., vol. 1 (Beirut, 1956), pp. 1143–44.
2. E. García Gómez, *Poemas arabigoandaluces* (Madrid, 1959), p. 45.
3. An interesting discussion of this parallel, seen from an orthodox Muslim's point of view, is found in Lois Giffen's book, *Theory of Profane Love among the Arabs: The Development of the Genre* (New York, 1971), p. 128.
4. E. García Gómez, *Un eclipse de la poesía en Sevilla: la época almorávide* (Madrid, 1945), p. 56.
5. See J. C. Vadet, *L'Esprit courtois en orient dans les cinq premiers siècles de l'Hégire* (Paris, 1968) for examples of this in the poetry of ᶜUmar ibn Abī Rabīᶜa.
6. An account of the Muslim tradition against gazing, along with other references to this motif, can be found in Lois Giffen, *Theory of Profane Love among the Arabs*, pp. 121–32.

CHAPTER FOUR

Basic Similarities

1. See above, Introduction, note 1.
2. For bibliographies, see Klaus Heger, "Die bisher veröffentlichten Harǧas und ihre Deutungen," *Beihefte zur Zeitschrift für romanische Philologie*, 101 (1960), and J. M. Solá-Solé, *Corpus de poesía mozárabe*.
3. García Gómez, *Las jarchas romances de la serie árabe en su marco*.
4. I did not have H. Nājī's edition of *Jaish al-Tawshīḥ* (Tunis, 1967) at my disposal while writing these chapters. Solá-Solé has noted many of the differences between García Gómez's edition and that of Nājī in *Corpus de poesía mozárabe*. Bilingual *muwashshaḥs* No. XXVII–No. XXXVIII in *Las jarchas romances* were found in this text by Ibn al-Khaṭīb.
5. A. Kh. Kinānī, *The Development of Gazal in Arabic Literature* (Damascus, 1951), p. 149.
6. Lois Giffen, *Theory of Profane Love Among the Arabs: The Development of the Genre* (New York, 1971), pp. 121–32.
7. I am using the same Roman numerals employed by García Gómez in *Las jarchas romances* to denote the bilingual *muwashshaḥs* from the manuscripts of Ibn Bushrā and Ibn al-Khaṭīb.

8. ᶜAlī ibn Ḥazm, *The Ring of the Dove*, trans, by A. J. Arberry (London, 1953), p. 9.
9. Kinānī, op. cit., pp. 157–58.
10. Ibn Ḥazm, op. cit., p. 82.
11. Alexander Denomy, *The Heresy of Courtly Love* (New York, 1947), pp. 47–48. There may also be traces of pre-Islamic paganism in images such as those involving the Kaaba. See J. C. Vadet, op. cit., pp. 445–51.
12. See M. F. Ghazi, "Un groupe social: 'Les Raffinés' (*Ẓurafā'*)," *Studia Islamica* XI (1959), pp. 39–71.
13. A study of this tradition has been made by J. C. Vadet, op. cit.
14. Ibn Ḥazm, op. cit., p. 220.
15. Kinānī, op. cit., p. 215.
16. The figure of the *raqīb* dates back to pre-Islamic times and is mentioned in the poetry of the period. See Vadet, op. cit., p. 59.
17. Ibn Ḥazm, op. cit., p. 105.
18. Ibid., p. 96.

CHAPTER FIVE

Differences Between the Last Stanzas

1. W. Wright, *A grammar of the Arabic Language*, 3d ed., vol. 2 (Cambridge, 1955), p. 214.
2. Ibid., p. 216.
3. Ibid., p. 217.
4. A. Hamori, "Examples of Convention in the Poetry of Abū Nuwās," *Studia Islamica*, XXX (1969), p. 11.
5. García Gómez, *Las jarchas romances*, pp. 112–13.
6. The *wāw* of *rubba* can also be observed in the last stanza of several Arabic *muwashshaḥs* which contain feminine *kharjas* of a popular type. Although these poems do not contain any Romance vocabulary, their structure is similar. For example, see Nos. 45, 66, 117, or 122 in *Jaish al-Tawshīḥ*, ed. by H. Nājī (Tunis, 1967).
7. García Gómez, "Dos nuevas jarŷas romances (XXV y XXVI) en muwaššahas árabes (MS. G. S. Colin)," *Al-Andalus*, XIX (1954), p. 371.
8. S. G. Armistead and J. H. Silverman, "La sanjuanada: ¿Huellas de una ḫarǧa mozárabe en la tradición actual?" *Nueva Revista de Filología Hispánica*, XVIII (1965–1966), pp. 436–43.
9. James T. Monroe, "Hispano-Arabic Poetry during the Almoravid Period: Theory and Practice," *Viator: Medieval and Renaissance Studies*, IV (1973), pp. 88–89.
10. Various *muwashshaḥs* which contain Arabic *kharjas* with similar women's verses may be part of the same literary tradition, shared by people throughout the Maghrib. Ibn Sanā' al-Mulk may have overlooked these examples when selecting his anthology because of his classical Eastern orientation. Further information about these Arabic *kharjas* can be found in an unpublished article by James T. Monroe, "The Arabic *Ḫarǧas* and their Relationship to Romance and to Colloquial Arabic Love Poetry of a Popular Type."

CHAPTER SIX

Arabic and Mozarabic *Kharjas*

1. Additional examples of *kharjas* with a young girl addressing her mother are found in the collections of Heger, op. cit., Solá-Solé, op cit., James T. Monroe, "Two New Bilingual *Ḫarǧas* (Arabic and Romance) in Arabic *Muwaššaḥs*," loc. cit., and "The Arabic *Ḫarǧas* and their Relationship to Romance and to Colloquial Arabic Love Poetry of a Popular Type" (unpublished paper).

2. S. M. Stern, *Hispano-Arabic Strophic Poetry*, p. 74.
3. The transliteration and translation were furnished by James T. Monroe.
4. Theodor Frings, *Minnesinger und Troubadours* (Berlin, 1949), and Peter Dronke, *Medieval Latin and the Rise of European Love-Lyric*, 2d ed., 2 vols. (Oxford, 1968).
5. *Kinānī*, op. cit., p. 219.
6. Ibid., p. 232.
7. Riad Malouf, *Les Chantres du Vin et de la Femme chez les Arabes*, (Paris, 1949), pp. 11–12.
8. Menéndez Pidal, "Cantos románicos andalusíes, continuadores de una lírica vulgar," *Boletín de la Real Academia Española*, XXXI (1951), pp. 241–44.
9. Beyond the confines of these two linguistic traditions, but within the context of Mediterranean civilization, where cultural patterns have overlapped for centuries, earlier examples of lyrics which are comparable to these *kharjas* have been found. Citing fragments of ancient Greek poets like Sappho, Anacreon, or Alcaeus, Elvira Gangutia Elícegui suggests that the motif of a young girl speaking to her mother stems from pagan sources which lost their sacred significance but continued to be cultivated in the form of secular lyrics throughout the Mediterranean region. In addition to Greek poetry, she cites evidence from Babylonia, Syria, Palestine, Phoenicia, and southern Italy. The possible link between the *kharjas* and this rich heritage merits further exploration. For details, see E. Gangutia Elícegui, "Poesía griega 'de amigo' y poesía arábigo-española," *Emerita*, XL (1972), pp. 329–96 and also James Monroe, "The Arabic *Ḫarǧas* and their Relationship to Romance and to Colloquial Arabic Love Poetry of a Popular Type."
10. Ibn Khaldūn, *Muqaddimah*, vol. 2, p. 305.
11. For more information about the *raqīb*, consult Chapter IV. Although the *raqīb* does not appear in *Dār al-Ṭirāz*, he has not been left out of the Arabic poems in *Jaish al-Tawshīḥ*. For example, see the *kharja* of *muwashshaḥ* No. 79 in *Jaish al-Tawshīḥ*, p. 111.
12. Other versions are given by Klaus Heger in "Die bisher veröffentlichten Ḫarǧas und ihre Deutungen," *Beihefte zur Zeitschrift für romanische Philologie*, 101, pp. 153–54, and by J. M. Solá-Solé in *Corpus de poesía mozárabe* (Barcelona, 1973), pp. 129–36.
13. Ibn Ḥazm, op. cit., p. 103.
14. Heger, op. cit., p. 153.
15. See E. Gangutia Elícegui, op. cit.
16. See Solá-Solé, *Corpus de poesía mozárabe*, pp. 138–39, for another interpretation of *khil(l)ello*.
17. The three consonants, *hā'*, *lām*, *shīn*, present a problem in No. XXXI, composed by Abū Bakr Muḥammad ibn Arfaᶜ Ra'suh during the mid-eleventh century. As far as we know, *g* before *i* did not evolve into an unvoiced fricative (roughly analogous to the Arabic unvoiced spirant, *hā'*) until the sixteenth century in the Spanish peninsula. Therefore, these three letters can not be a transliteration of the Romance form, *gilos* (jealous one). Nevertheless, in the course of scribal transmission of the Romance words in the *kharjas* by Arabic-speaking copyists, almost any alterations of the original words are possible. On this premise, the initial *hā'* of the word might conceivably have been a misreading of a *jīm*, which accurately would have rendered the medieval *g* before *i*, namely a combination of a voiced dental stop and a voiced palatal sibilant (dž), as in No. III and No. XXVII. Another possibility, which is always present in this field, is that an error may have been made in translating this word. This alternative is supported by Solá-Solé, who gives an entirely different rendition of the last line of this *kharja* (op. cit., pp. 281–84).
18. A. B. Lord, *The Singer of Tales* (Cambridge, 1964), p. 49.
19. For a discussion of pre-Christian aspects, see E. Gangutia Elícegui, "Poesía griega 'de amigo' y poesía arabigo-española," *Emérita*, XL (1972), pp. 329–96.
20. See Menéndez Pidal, "Cantos románicos," loc. cit., pp. 187–270 and M. Frenk Alatorre, "Jarŷas mozárabes," loc. cit., pp. 281–84.
21. A. B. Lord, *Singer of Tales*, p. 130.
22. García Gómez, *Las jarchas romances*, pp. 194–95. See Solá-Solé, op. cit., pp. 97–101 for a variant reading.

23. García Gómez, *Las jarchas romances*, pp. 136–37. If Solá-Solé's interpretation is correct, then only the assonance would remain, for he replaces the second *non* with *yo*. See above, note 16.
24. Ibid., pp. 244–45. Concerning St. John's day, see Dozy, *Supplément aux Dictionnaires*, vol. 2 (Leiden–Paris, 1927), p. 181, along with Chapter V, notes 7, 8, and 9 above.
25. García Gómez, *Las jarchas romances*, pp. 364–65.
26. Ibid., pp. 130–31. Consult Solá-Solé for variant readings, op. cit., pp. 193–99.
27. The transliterations given in Heger, op. cit., p. 139, for the word García Gómez transcribes as *kita* in *Las jarchas romances*, pp. 156–57, are *kry*, taken from García Gomez's first interpretation, and *fry*, taken from Stern's collection. Other possible readings, therefore, might be *quiere* or *farey* (*haré*). See Solá-Solé, op. cit., pp. 305–7 also.
28. Repetition is also found in some of the colloquial Arabic *kharjas* in *Jaish al-Tawshīḥ*.
29. See Bernard Lewis and S. M. Stern in *Eos: An Enquiry into the Theme of Lovers' Meetings and Partings at Dawn in Poetry*, ed. by A. T. Hatto (The Hague, 1965), pp. 215–22.
30. E. M. Wilson and S. M. Stern in *Eos: An Enquiry into the Theme of Lovers' Meetings and Partings at Dawn in Poetry*, pp. 299–321.
31. J. S. Révah, "Note sur le mot 'matrana,'" *Al-Andalus*, XVIII (1953), p. 148.
32. The diverse interpretations of this can be found in Solá-Solé, op. cit., pp. 285–88.
33. García Gómez, "Estudio del *Dār aṭ-Ṭirāz*," loc. cit., p. 89.
34. García Gómez, *Las jarchas romances*, pp. 124–25.
35. Phonic interference also occurs in bilingual situations, but due to the fact that I do not know exactly how either the Arabic in Spain or the Mozarabic dialect sounded, nor do I know if the Arabic letters being used to record Romance words in the *kharjas* were pronounced in an identical manner by the indigenous singers, I do not believe that I could make any accurate observations about phonic values at this time.
36. My commentary is based on the transliterations of García Gómez. Another reading of the texts might result in different interpretations. For example, Solá-Solé reads *ad union* instead of *adúname* in No. XXXV.
37. *Fen* is the equivalent of *ven* in modern Spanish.
38. García Gómez, *Las jarchas romances*, p. 321. The interpretation of *huyda* here is questionable. *F* did not become *h* in Castilian until much later. Furthermore, the Mozarabic dialect was spoken in al-Andalus, not in Castile. Solá-Solé has taken this into account in his version of the text, op. cit., pp. 142–43.
39. García Gómez, *Las jarchas romances*, p. 264.
40. Although Solá-Solé's interpretation is different, the word, *alma*, is repeated twice, op. cit., pp. 305–7.
41. See G. Weil, "ᶜAruḍ," *Encyclopaedia of Islam*, New Edition, vol. 1 (London, 1960), pp. 667–77.
42. Wright, *A Grammar of the Arabic Language*, vol. 2, p. 356.
43. The complete rhyme words of the *maṭlaᶜ* and *kharja* of *muwashshaḥ* No. 1 are as follows: *jumān, badrī, zamān, ṣadrī*, and *ᶜayyān, tadrī, zamān, dhikrī*, respectively.
44. Although Solá-Solé's interpretation is different from that of García Gómez in this case, the final rhyme is the same in the different readings, gathered together in *Corpus de poesía mozárabe*, pp. 141–44.
45. Because *maṭlaᶜ* is a technical name for the *qufl* which precedes the first *bait* of a *muwashshaḥ*, it will often be simpler to refer to both the *maṭlaᶜ* and the *qufls* of a poem with the one word, *qufl*. Both terms are unnecessary when I refer to all the *qufls* of a *muwashshaḥ* in a generalized manner.
46. There are alternative interpretations for this *kharja*, indicated in note 27 of this chapter.
47. Solá-Solé reads *legárte* instead of *férte*, op. cit., p. 117. This still produces a posttonic rhyme with *nókhte*.
48. I would like to indicate that a *kharja* with Romance words at the line's end does not necessarily have to contain rhyme. Nevertheless, if only an Arabic rhyme can be seen in its last syllables, then I would consider the *kharja* to be deviant.

49. The number should be reduced to six if the *kharjas* with self-rhyming words are deemed acceptable possibilities by the reader.
50. García Gómez, "Estudio del *Dār aṭ-Ṭirāz*," loc. cit., p. 96.
51. G. Weil, "ᶜArud," loc. cit., p. 676.
52. James Monroe has located Spanish metrical equivalents to many Arabic *kharjas* in his study, "The Arabic *Ḫarǧas* and their Relationship to Romance and to Colloquial Arabic Love Poetry of a Popular Type."
53. Although this thesis does not concern itself with the Hebrew *muwashshaḥs*, Jewish culture must not be overlooked when considering the environment of al-Andalus during the Middle Ages.
54. Ibn Khaldūn, *The Muqaddimah*, vol. 3, p. 413.
55. A discussion of the *muwashshaḥ*'s diffusion throughout North Africa and the Middle East is found in S. M. Stern, *Hispano–Arabic Strophic Poetry*, pp. 67–80.

APPENDIX

Historical Background: A Brief Sketch

1. For example, the late S. M. Stern indicated that Ibn Bassām's information should be considered more reliable in *Hispano–Arabic Strophic Poetry*, pp. 63–66. Brian Dutton and James Monroe, on the other hand, think that the name given by Ibn Khaldūn is probably correct. See Brian Dutton, "Some New Evidence for the Romance Origins of the *Muwashshaḥas*," *Bulletin of Hispanic Studiss*, XLII (1965), pp. 78–81, and James T. Monroe, "Hispano–Arabic Poetry During the Caliphate of Cordoba: Theory and Practice," loc. cit., pp. 133–34, note 26.
2. Ibn Bassām al-Shantarīnī, *Al-Dhakhīrah fī Maḥāsin Ahl al-Jazīrah*, vol. 1, pp. 1–2. This name was probably taken from an earlier work by ᶜUbāda ibn Mā' al-Samā', according to Stern, *Hispano–Arabic Strophic Poetry*, pp. 63–66.
3. Ibn Khaldūn, *Muqaddimah*, vol. 3, p. 440. He is believed to have copied this information from Ibn Saᶜīd. See Stern's *Hispano–Arabic Strophic Poetry* for a detailed account of the history of these source materials.
4. Ibn Khaldūn, *Muqaddimah*, vol. 3, p. 441.
5. Muṣṭafā al-Karīm, *Fann al-Tawshīḥ* (Beirut, 1959), p. 100.
6. Ibid., p. 110.
7. Ibid., p. 56.
8. Ibid., p. 44.
9. A. R. Nykl, *Hispano–Arabic Poetry and Its Relations with the Old Provençal Troubadours* (Baltimore, 1946), p. 269.
10. Al-Karīm, op. cit., p. 51.
11. García Gomez, "Una pre-muwaššaḥa atribuida a Abū Nuwās," *Al-Andalus*, XXI (1956), pp. 406–22.
12. Iḥsān ᶜAbbās, *Tarīkh al-Adab al-Andalusī* (Beirut, 1960), pp. 35–37.
13. Al-Karīm, op. cit., p. 51.
14. ᶜAbbās, op. cit., pp. 97–98.
15. Al-Karīm, op. cit., p. 95.
16. Ibid., p. 87.
17. Philip K. Hitti, *History of the Arabs*, 7th ed. (New York, 1961), p. 515. See also M. F. Ghazi, op. cit., pp. 39–71.
18. Ibn Khaldūn, *Muqaddimah*, vol. 2, p. 405.
19. Hitti, op. cit., p. 598.
20. Al-Karīm, op. cit., p. 88.
21. ᶜAbbās, op. cit., p. 40.
22. Abū ᶜUthmān ᶜAmr ibn Baḥr al-Jāḥiẓ, *Kitāb al-Bayān wa al-Tabyīn* (Cairo, 1948), p. 385.

23. García Gómez, "Estudio del *Dār aṭ-Ṭirāz*," loc. cit., p. 55.
24. B. Dutton, op. cit.
25. J. T. Monroe, "Hispano–Arabic Poetry during the Caliphate of Cordoba," loc. cit.
26. Concerning the possibility of Latin influence, which should be taken into consideration, Peter Dronke comments:

> But though this ryhthmic pattern, or something very near it, can be traced in liturgical Latin to the beginnings of the Mozarabic period, and probably existed even earlier . . . how could we ever be sure that such things began in Latin and were not borrowed from traditional songs of the people (and then returned)? As far back as we can go, church and court and people exist side by side, and in a thousand ways, mostly incalculable, their poetry and songs are shared (op. cit., vol. 1, p. 263).

27. "El libro de Alexandre," in *Poetas castellanos anteriores al siglo XV*, Biblioteca de Autores Españoles, vol. 57 (Madrid, 1952), p. 147.
28. García Gómez, "Estudio del *Dār aṭ-Ṭirāz*," loc. cit., p. 96.
29. Al-Karīm, op. cit., p. 108.
30. Pierre le Gentil, "La strophe zadjalesque, les khardjas et le problème des origines du lyrisme roman," *Romania*, LXXIV (1963), pp. 1–27, 209–50.
31. Buṭrus al-Bustānī, *Udabā' al-^{c}Arab fī al-Andalus wa ^{c}Asr al-Inbi^{c}āth*, 3d ed. (Beirut, 1937), pp. 80–81. Nevertheless, he does not specify which genres of jongleurs' songs he means nor their place of origin. This is confusing because the medieval Castilian epic, with its assonant rhyme and irregular meter, differed from examples of medieval lyrics with consonant rhymes and counted syllables which have been preserved. The *kharjas*, clearly, form part of a lyrical tradition.
32. Iḥsān ^{c}Abbās in *Al-Muwashshaḥāt al-Andalusiyya* (Beirut, 1964), p. 7.
33. Menéndez Pidal, "Cantos románicos," loc. cit., pp. 266–67.
34. Leo Spitzer, *Linguística e historia literaria*, 2d ed. (Madrid, 1961), p. 86.
35. Margit Frenk Alatorre, op. cit., p. 284.
36. H. G. Farmer, *A History of Arabian Music to the XIIIth Century* (London, 1929), pp. 52–53.
37. Abū al-Faraj al-Iṣbahānī, *Kitāb al-Aghāni*, vol. 8 (Cairo, 1963), pp. 321–22.
38. Farmer, op. cit., pp. 78–79.
39. Al-Iṣbahānī, op. cit., vol. 1, pp. 378–79.
40. Iḥsān ^{c}Abbās in *Al-Muwashshaḥāt al-Andalusiyya*, p. 5.
41. Farmer, op. cit., p. 81.
42. G. E. von Grunebaum, "'Lírica románica' before the Arab Conquest," *Al-Andalus*, XXI (1956), p. 404.
43. Ibid., p. 405.
44. Muḥammad ibn Isḥāq ibn al-Nadīm, *The Fihrist of al-Nadīm*, trans. by Bayard Dodge (New York, 1970), pp. 643–44.
45. Al-Ḥulw, *Al-Muwashshaḥāt al-Andalusiyya*, p. 32.
46. Farmer, op. cit., pp. 126–27.
47. Al-Karīm, op. cit., p. 85.
48. Ibid., p. 18.
49. Ibn Khaldūn, *Muqaddimah*, vol. 3, p. 454.

Selected Bibliography

ᶜAbbās, Iḥsān, *Ṯarīkh al-Adab al-Andalusī*, Beirut, 1960.

Alatorre, Margit Frenk. "Jarŷas mozárabes y estribillos franceses," *Nueva Revista de Filología Hispánica* VI, 1952, 281–84.

ᶜAlī ibn Ḥusayn, Abū al-Faraj al-Iṣbahānī, *Kitāb al-Aghānī*. Vols. 1 and 8. Cairo, 1963.

Alonso, Dámaso. "Cancioncillas 'de amigo' mozárabes." *Revista de Filología Española* XXXIII, 1949, 297–349.

Anīs, Ibrāhīm. *Mūsīqā al-Shiᶜr*. Cairo, 1965.

Armistead, S. G. and J. H. Silverman. "La sanjuanada: ¿Huellas de una ḫarğa mozárabe en la tradición actual?" *Nueva Revista de Filología Hispánica* XVIII, 1965–66, 436–43.

Al-Bustānī, Buṭrus. *Udabā' al-ᶜArab fī al-Andalus wa ᶜAsr al-Inbiᶜāth*. 3d ed. Beirut, 1937.

Cantera, Francisco. *La canción mozárabe*. Santander, 1957.

Denomy, Alexander J. *The Heresy of Courtly Love*. New York, 1947.

Dozy, R. *Supplément aux dictionaires arabes*. 2 vols. Leiden–Paris, 1927.

Dronke, Peter. *Medieval Latin and the Rise of European Love-Lyric*. 2d ed. 2 vols. Oxford, 1968.

Dutton, Brian. "Some New Evidence for the Romance Origins of the *Muwashshaḥas*," *Bulletin of Hispanic Studies* XLII, 1965.

Encyclopaedia of Islam. 4 vols. and supplement. Leiden, 1913–38.

Encyclopaedia of Islam. New edition. Leiden, 1954– .

Farmer, Henry George. *A History of Arabian Music to the XIIIth Century*. London, 1929.

Frings, Theodor. *Minnesinger und Troubadours*. Berlin, 1949.

Gangutia Elícegui, Elvira. "Poesía griega 'de amigo' y poesía arábigo-española," *Emerita* XL, 1972, 329–96.

García Gómez, Emilio. "Sobre el nombre y la patria del autor de la muwaššaḥa." *Al-Andalus* II, 1934, 215–22.

———. *Un eclipse de la poesía en Sevilla: la época almorávide*. Madrid, 1945.

———. "Veintecuatro jarŷas romances en muwaššaḥas árabes." *Al-Andalus*, XVII 1952, pp. 57–127.

———. "Dos neuvas jarŷas romances (XXV y XXVI) en muwaššaḥas árabes (MS. G. S. Colin)." *Al-Andalus* XIX, 1954, 369–91.

———. "La 'Ley de Mussafia' se aplica a la poesía estrófica arabigoandaluza." *Al-Andalus* XXVII, 1962, 1–20.

———. *Las jarchas romances de la serie árabe en su marco*. Madrid, 1965.

———. "Estudio del *Dār aṭ-Ṭirāz*." *Al-Andalus* XXVII, 1962, 28–104.

———. "Una pre-muwaššaḥa atribuida a Abū Nuwās." *Al-Andalus* XXI, 1956, 406–14.

Ghazi, M. F. "Un groupe social: 'Les Raffinés' (*Ẓurafā'*)." *Studia Islamica* XI, 1959, 39–71.

Gibb, H. A. R. *Arabic Literature.* 2d ed. Oxford, 1963.

Giffen, Lois. *Theory of Profane Love among the Arabs: The Development of the Genre.* New York, 1971.

Hamori, A. "Examples of Convention in the Poetry of Abū Nuwās." *Studia Islamica* XXX, 1969, 5–26.

Hartmann, Martin. *Das Arabische Strophengedicht. I. Das Muwaššaḥ.* Weimar, 1897.

Hatto, A. T., ed. *Eos: An Enquiry into the Theme of Lovers' Meetings and Partings at Dawn in Poetry.* The Hague, 1965.

Heger, Klaus. "Die bisher veröffentlichten Harǧas und ihre Deutungen." *Beihefte zur Zeitschrift für romanische Philologie* 101, 1960.

Hitti, Philip K. *History of the Arabs.* 7th ed. New York, 1961.

Hornik, Marcel P., ed. *Collected Studies in Honor of Américo Castro's Eightieth Year.* Oxford, 1965.

Al-Ḥulw, Salīm. *Al-Muwashshaḥāt al-Andalusiyya.* Preface by Iḥsān ᶜAbbās. Beirut, 1965.

Ibn Ḥazm. *The Ring of the Dove.* Trans. by A. J. Arberry. London, 1953.

Ibn Khaldūn. *The Muqaddimah.* Trans. by Franz Rosenthal, 3 vols. New York, 1958.

Ibn Khaldūn, Tarīkh al-ᶜAllāmah. Ed. by Y. A. Dāghir. 2d ed. Vol. 1. Beirut, 1956.

Ibn al-Khaṭīb, Lisān al-Dīn. *Jaish al-Tawshīḥ.* Ed. by Hilāl Nājī. Tunis, 1967.

Ibn al-Nadīm, Muḥammad ibn Isḥāq. *The Fihrist of al-Nadīm.* Trans. by Bayard Dodge. New York, 1970.

Ibn Sanā' al-Mulk. *Dār al-Ṭirāz.* Ed. by Jawdat Rikābi, Damascus, 1949.

al-Jāḥiz, ᶜAmr ibn Baḥr. *Al-Bayān wa al-Tabyīn.* Ed. by ᶜAbd al-Salām Hārūn. Vol. 1, part 1. Cairo, 1948.

Al-Karīm, Mustafā. *Fann al-Tawshīḥ.* Beirut, 1959.

Kinānī, A. Kh. *The Development of Gazal in Arabic Literature.* Damascus, 1951.

Le Gentil, Pierre. "La strophe zadjalesque, les khardjas et le problème des origines du lyrisme roman." *Romania* LXXXIV, 1963, 1–27, 209–50.

Levy, Reuben. *The Social Structure of Islam.* New York, 1965.

Lord, A. B. *The Singer of Tales.* Cambridge, 1964.

Malouf, Riad. *Les chantres du vin et de la femme chez les arabes.* Paris, 1949.

Menéndez Pidal, Ramón. "Cantos románicos andalusíes, continuadores de una lírica vulgar." *Boletín de la Real Academia Española* XXXI, 1951, 187–270.

———. *Orígenes del Español.* 2d ed. Madrid, 1929.

Monroe, James. *Hispano–Arabic Poetry.* Berkeley, 1974.

———. "Hispano–Arabic Poetry During the Almoravid Period: Theory and Practice." Viator: *Medieval and Renaissance Studies* IV, 1973, 65–98.

———. "Two New Bilingual *Harǧas* (Arabic and Romance) in Arabic *Muwaššaḥs*." *Hispanic Review* XLII, 1974.

Nykl, A. R. *Hispano–Arabic Poetry and its Relations with the Old Provençal Troubadours.* Baltimore, 1946.

Poetas castellanos anteriores al siglo XV. Biblioteca de Autores Españoles. Vol. 57. Madrid, 1952.

Révah, J. S. "Note sur le mot 'matrana'." *Al-Andalus* XVIII, 1953, 148.

Ribera y Tarragó, Julián. *Disertaciones y opúsculos.* 2 vols. Madrid, 1928.

———. *Historia de la música árabe medieval y su influencia en la española.* Madrid, 1927.

Al-Shantarīnī, Abū al-Ḥasan ᶜAlī ibn Bassām. *Al-Dhakhīrah fī Maḥāsin Ahl al-Jazīrah.* Ed. by Ṭāhā Ḥusayn. 3 vols. Cairo, 1939–45.

Saporta, Sol, ed. *Psycholinguistics.* New York, 1961.

Solá-Solé, J. M. *Corpus de Poesía Mozárabe.* Barcelona, 1973.

Spitzer, Leo. *Linguística e historia literaria.* 2d ed. Madrid, 1961.

Steiger, A. *Contribución a la fonética del hispano–árabe y de los arabismos en el ibero–románico y el siciliano.* Madrid, 1932.

Stern, S. M. "Les Vers finaux en espagnol dans les muwaššaḥs hispano–hebraïques." *Al-Andalus* XIII, 1948, 299–346.

———. "Studies on Ibn Quzmān." *Al-Andalus* XVI, 1951, 379–425.
———. "Two Anthologies of Muwaššaḥ poetry: Ibn al-Ḫaṭib's *Ǧayš al-tawšīḥ* and al-Ṣafadī's *Tawšīᶜ al-tawšīḥ*." *Arabica* II, 1955, 150–92.
———. "Four Famous Muwaššaḥs from Ibn Bushrā's Anthology." *Al-Andalus* XXIII, 1958, 339–69.
———. *Hispano–Arabic Strophic Poetry*. Ed. by L. P. Harvey. Oxford, 1974.
———. *Les chansons mozarabes*. Oxford, 1964.
Vadet, Jean-Claude. *L'Esprit courtois en orient dans les cinq premiers siècles de l'Hégire*. Paris, 1968.
Von Grunebaum, G. E., ed. *Arabic Poetry*. Wiesbaden, 1973.
———. "'Lírica románica' before the Arab Conquest." *Al-Andalus* XXI, 1956, 403–5.
———. *Medieval Islam*. Chicago, 1961.
Weil, Gotthold. "ᶜArud." *Encyclopaedia of Islam*. New Edition. Vol. 1. Leiden, 1960, 667–77.
Wright, W. *A Grammar of the Arabic Language*. 3d ed. Revised by Robertson Smith and M. J. de Goeje. 2 vols. Cambridge, 1955.

Index

Titles of works are not indexed.

Reference is by author's name only.